Rest Camps of the Kruger Park

The Southern 3

Skukuza, Pretoriuskop, and Lower Sabie

Rest Camps of the Kruger Park

The Southern 3

Skukuza, Pretoriuskop, and Lower Sabie

2017 EDITION

Marius J. Smook

Rest Camps of the Kruger Park —The Southern 3 — Skukuza, Pretoriuskop, and Lower Sabie

Published by:

Smook Books LLC for Kruger Kids
18801 N. Dale Mabry Hwy., Suite 552,
Lutz, FL 433548
USA
www.KrugerKids.org
KrugerKidsSafaris@Gmail.com

First printed in 2017

ISBN-13: 978-1544723792

ISBN-10: 1544723792

10 9 8 7 6 5 4 3 2 1

Dedication

This book is dedicated to the past, current and future Kruger National Park staff members and the South African Government. Without their foresight, dedication, commitment, perseverance and hard work, we would not have the gift of being able to still see Africa as it looked before the advent of modern civilisation.

2018 Edition –
Be a "Meerkat" Book Contributor

Rest Camps of the Kruger Park is an ongoing project. The author intends its 5 volumes, plus 2 Bushveld Camp volumes, to evolve and improve with each annual edition.

To make this happen, lovers of the Kruger National Park are invited to be a part of the journey by being "Meerkat" Book Contributors. If, when visiting a rest camp, you are always on the lookout, just like the meerkat, then you will notice mistakes in this book, ways to improve, or have suggestions. If so, please send an email to KrugerKidsSafaris@gmail.com and let the author know about it.

All contributions will be acknowledged in the next edition after the contribution is made.

The author is particularly in need of the following contributions for the 2018 edition:

- More camp photos
- Accommodation interior photos
- Interesting wildlife sighting photos in and from the camps
- Good camp tips and cautions
- Photos of evening bush braais
- Photos taken on night game drives
- Accommodation reviews
- Interesting trivia or historical facts about the camps
- Camp amenity reviews
- Rest camp stories

Acknowledgements of rest camp staff members, who so often go out of their way to make our Kruger experiences so magical, will also be welcomed and their conduct acknowledged.

Please consider becoming a "Meerkat" Book Contributor and help the author share the gift of the *Rest Camps of the Kruger National Park* with the world.

Table of Contents

Other Volumes

REST CAMPS OF THE KRUGER PARK

Featuring the twelve main rest camps and their five satellites.
What to expect, do, and see, plus where to sleep, eat, and how to get there.

THE NORTHERN 3
• Letaba • Olifants • Balule

In support of
KRUGER KIDS
Giving orphan kids the gift of a Kruger Safari.

2017 Edition
Marius J. Smook

REST CAMPS OF THE KRUGER PARK

Featuring the twelve main rest camps and their five satellites.
What to expect, do, and see, plus where to sleep, eat, and how to get there.

THE LOWER-SOUTH 3
• Berg-en-Dal • Malelane • Crocodile Bridge

In support of
KRUGER KIDS
Giving orphan kids the gift of a Kruger Safari.

2017 Edition
Marius J. Smook

REST CAMPS OF THE KRUGER PARK

Featuring the twelve main rest camps and their five satellites.
What to expect, do, and see, plus where to sleep, eat, and how to get there.

THE CENTRAL 4
• Satara • Orpen • Maroela • Tamboti

In support of
KRUGER KIDS
Giving orphan kids the gift of a Kruger Safari.

2017 Edition
Marius J. Smook

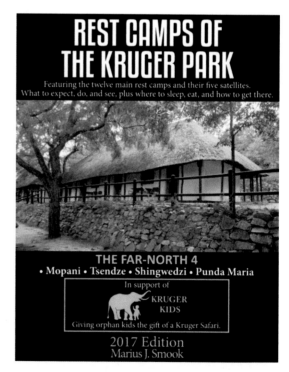

REST CAMPS OF THE KRUGER PARK

Featuring the twelve main rest camps and their five satellites.
What to expect, do, and see, plus where to sleep, eat, and how to get there.

THE FAR-NORTH 4
• Mopani • Tsendze • Shingwedzi • Punda Maria

In support of
KRUGER KIDS
Giving orphan kids the gift of a Kruger Safari.

2017 Edition
Marius J. Smook

Acknowledgements

The author wishes to thank and credit the following people and entities for their contribution to the publishing of this book:

SANParks for the outstanding way that they sustain and develop the Kruger National Park for the pleasure, education and benefit of all South African citizens and international visitors alike.

The Kruger National Park employees listed below for assisting with the animal, bird, and tree species listed in this book:
Bishop Adonia — Shingwedzi Camp Head Field Guide
John Adamson — Letaba Camp Head Field Guide
Dennis Mokoena — Olifants Camp Head Field Guide
Edward Ndhlovu — Satara Camp Head Field Guide
Stephen Midzi — Pretoriuskop Camp Section Ranger
Peter Zitha — Berg-en-Dal Camp Head Field Guide
Erving Knight — Crocodile Bridge Head Field Guide
Amos Gazide — Mopani Camp Head Field Guide
Garth Holt — Punda Maria Camp Manager
Tsakani Chabalala — Orpen Camp Junior Field Guide
Michele Hofmeyr — Skukuza Indigenous Nursery Manager
Thank you also to:
Aitken Makhense — People in Conservation Manager — for introducing the author to the School Journey Program as well as for helping him locate suitable children's accommodations for the Kruger Kids Program.
Intumeleng Khadambi — Archive Manager — for helping the author to research the history of the rest camps at Skukuza Library.
The many camp administration and reception staff members — who always provided the author with friendly and helpful assistance whenever requested.

SANParks is credited for the park map, rest camp perimeter and road outlines — SANParks.org
Adobe Stock is credited for many of the animal and bird images — Stock.adobe.com

Furthermore, a special thank you to the professionals listed below for their support of the Kruger Kids project by contributing an enormous amount of their time and skills to edit, proofread, and create the maps for this book. The author highly recommends their services, and readers who need similar services are encouraged to support them. Their direct contact details can be accessed at www.KrugerKids.org/Acknowledgements:

Colleen Hughes, a MA graduate in Education & Development from the University of Sussex, contributed to this publication through proofreading.
Sara Robinson, a multidisciplinary Rhodes University and Stellenbosch University graduate, contributed to this book with her copy-editing and proofreading skills.
Elize Loubser (Clasina Elizabeth Fourie), a B.Sc. and M.Sc. in Zoology graduate from the University of Pretoria (Mammal Research Institute) and the University of the Free State respectively, contributed her zoological expertise and editing strengths to this book.
Erin French, a Bachelor of English senior at Texas State University, contributed to this book with her strengths in editing and writing.
Cassandra Raposo, a Bachelor of English Writing, Rhetoric, and Communications graduate of the University of Massachusetts Dartmouth also contributed her strengths in editing and writing.
Pamela Beltowski, a Bachelor of Graphic Design graduate from The Art Institute of Pittsburgh contributed her skill of innovative thinking and pristine detail to this book.
Lauren Pronger, a Haverford College double major in Linguistics and Computer Sciences contributed her proofreading skills to this book.

Finally, the author would like to thank his wife **Lize**, daughter **Kylah**, son **Keaton**, and **Nisa Gonzalez** for their support and help during the three years that it took to produce all 5 volumes of *Rest Camps of the Kruger Park*.

Bushveld Store

Here you will find everything that you need to make your visit to the Kruger National Park enjoyable. Included are cameras, binoculars, torches, guide books, maps, safari gear, and much more.

All prices are exactly the same as you will find when you go directly to buy online from Amazon.com. However, by purchasing via this store, our Kruger Kids project earns a small commission from every sale. If there is something which you need that you do not see here, please let us know so that we can add it to make this a great, one-stop for all of your Kruger safari needs.

Visit our store at
BushveldStore.com

South African customers please note that all goods are supplied from the United States or Europe and delivery is guaranteed by Amazon.com via private courier services. Aside from this benefit, and the advantage of a wide selection, comparing prices will more often than not reveal that they are most competitive.

In support of

KRUGER
KIDS

Giving orphaned children the gift of a Kruger safari

Rest Camps of the Kruger Park

The Southern 3

Skukuza, Pretoriuskop, and Lower Sabie

How To Use The Maps In This Book

Overview map:

The first map that you will see in each chapter is the *General Overview Map*. **This map is intended to display only a simple overview of the camp.** It shows the bare essentials of what you need to know if you are planning to stay overnight, or are a day-visitor to the camp.

When planning to stay overnight, by referring to the colour-coded areas, you can quickly see where your party size may be accommodated. For example, if you are a party of 3 people, then the ▢ area which offers 3-sleeper units will be of interest to you. If you are planning to camp, then you will focus on the ▮ area.

For day-visitors, the *General Overview Map* shows appropriate icons for the public toilet, observation area, shop, restaurant, petrol station, museum, and reception.

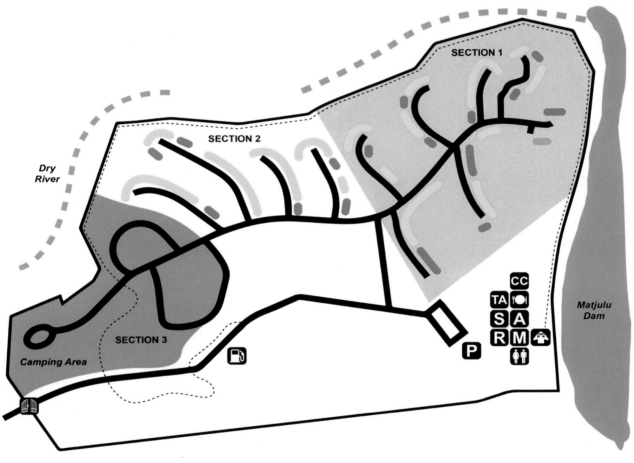

Overview Map Key			
▢ 3-sleepers	▢ 6-sleepers	▢ 8-12 sleeper	▮ Campsite
A Auditorium	**M** Museum	**R** Reception	🚹🚺 Toilets
S Shop	🍽 Restaurant	⛺ Observation	**P** Parking
⛩ Gate	⛽ Petrol	**CC** Conference	⋯⋯ Walk route

Section maps:

Unlike *Overview Maps*, **Section Maps show accommodation details**. Numbered icons provide important facts about views and the bathing, toilet, and cooking facilities for each unit. **Also shown are the location of overnight-guest communal amenities**, such as bathrooms, kitchens, laundries, and pools.

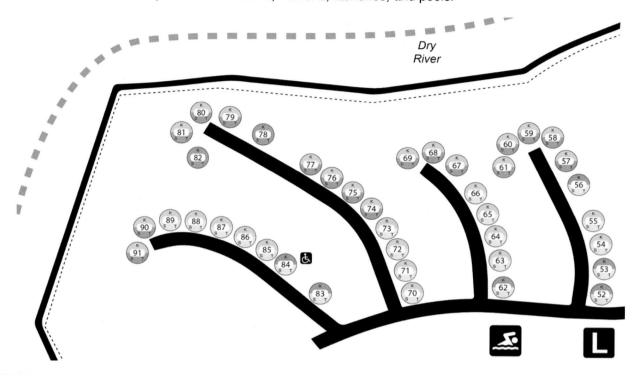

Accommodation icons:

Icon shapes indicate if an accommodation unit is either a safari tent, bungalow/hut/cottage, or guest house:

Tent   Bungalow/ hut/cottage   Guest house

The top half of each icon is sleeper colour-coded in the same number and sleeper colours as in the *Overview Map*:

1-sleeper unit   2-sleeper unit   3-sleeper unit   4-sleeper unit

The bottom half of each icon is colour-coded to indicate the unit's view:

Water view   Perimeter view   No view   Perimeter and water view

Most icons also include the letters "K", "S", and "T", which indicate a unit's self-catering, bathing, and toilet facilities:

The "K" icon means: In-unit, self-catering facilities such as a kitchen, kitchenette, or hot plate with cooking utensils, cutlery and crockery.

The "T" means: In-unit toilet(s), either en-suite or sharing.
The "S" means: In-unit washing facilities, such as a bath or shower, either en-suite or sharing.

Accommodation unit pictures:

Below each detailed section map, you will see pictures of the accommodation units represented on the map by the individual icons. Here are some examples:

2-sleeper bungalow — Code BG2

6-sleeper family cottage — Code FF6D

2-sleeper safari tent — Code ST2

2-sleeper hut — Code EB2

Accommodation unit numbers:

The South African National Parks (SANParks) use a system of codes to refer to the different accommodations. The tables below include these codes for easy reference when reading the maps shown on the SANParks official website https://www.sanparks.org/parks/kruger or when making reservations online or by phone. Also included is a table of unit numbers with their corresponding codes as per the example below:

Codes	Unit numbers
BA3	4–10,3–16,20,21,33–35,41–43,45,46
BA3U	27,28, 29–32,37–39
BA3UZ	23–25
FA6	1–3,11,12,17–19,22,26,36,40,44,47,83,84

Accommodation details:

Below the pictures, the Accommodation Details Tables show all of the in-unit details for each type of accommodation, identified by the same colour-coded icons shown on the detailed Section Maps. There you will see exactly how many rooms, beds, the type of bathing, toilet, and self-catering facilities that are offered.

Below is an example of an Accommodation Details Table.

Bungalow and family cottage details (See detail map)			
Icons	Unit	Unit	Unit
Booking codes	BA3	BA3U	FA6
Type	Bungalow	Bungalow	Fam. cot.
Number of units	34	34 + 1	28+1
Wheelchair-accessible units		1	1
Wheelchair-accessible unit		BA3UZ	FA6Z
Perimeter view	•	•	
Base guests allowance	2	2	4
Minimum rate	R1,075	R1,075	R1,960
Maximum rate	R1,330	R1,330	R2,490
Minimum additional adult rate	R240	R240	R410
Maximum additional adult rate	R260	R260	R430
Additional child discount	50%	50%	50%
Maximum beds/people	3	3	6
3 single beds	•	•	
2 single beds			•
Sep. bedroom with double bed			•
2 bench-couches in lounge			•
Toilet and shower	•	•	•
Toilet and bath		•	•
Utensils	•	•	•
Fridge	•	•	•
Hot plate	•	•	•
Sink/Basin	•	•	•
Air-conditioned	•	•	•
Fan			•
Electric points	•	•	•
Non-smoking	•	•	•

Unit location tips:

Finally, to further help you to reserve the best accommodation unit that suits your preferences, we have included a table of location tips, as per the example below:

Bungalow location tips	
Best perimeter/river views	23–30,32
Quietest	23–32,37–40,48–50,58–60,68,69
Closest to the pool	52,62,70
Closest to the shop/restaurant	1–5
Closest to the laundromat	52,62
Best perimeter/river views	23–30,32

Disclaimer

This publication, the publisher, author, and the Kruger Kids project are not part of, affiliated to, associated with, or in any way endorsed by the Kruger National Park or SANParks.

The rates, prices, travel distances, times, weather data, accommodation locations, or any other facts contained in this book are for illustrative purposes only and are not guaranteed to be accurate.

The information contained in this book should only be used as a rough guide to planning a Kruger Park visit.

THE CAMP FACILITIES AND AMENITIES ARE CONTINUALLY BEING UPGRADED. THEREFORE, YOU MUST TREAT THE DATA CONTAINED IN THIS BOOK AND ITS SUBSEQUENT EDITIONS AS EVOLVING INFORMATION ONLY. BEFORE MAKING ANY DECISIONS ABOUT VISITING ANY OF THE CAMPS, CONFIRM THAT YOUR ACCOMMODATION AND AMENITY NEEDS CAN BE MET.

You can do this by either of the options below:

1) Referring to the data and interior images of each unit type via the *Tariffs* tab for each camp in the SANParks official website https://www.sanparks.org. The data and images can also be easily accessed via the web links at the bottom of the *accommodation details tables* in each rest camp chapter in this book.

2) Confirming with camp reception offices by phone or email.

3) Paying close attention to the SANParks website (https://www.sanparks.org/bookings) reservation pages when you book your trip.

The author is not a field guide, safari professional, tour guide, or travel agent. Any travel, fauna and flora spotting, or other suggestions, tips or cautions given in this book are the author's own opinions based on his own experience, observations and conclusions.

You should always make contact with and seek the advice of a professional travel agent, the SANParks or camp reception offices and personnel before acting on anything read in this book and when planning to visit the Kruger Park.

Some of the material in this book includes links to third party information, opinions, and more, which are all their own and may or may not be accurate. As such, the author does not assume responsibility or liability for any third party material.

Users of this guide are advised to do their own research when it comes to making decisions about visiting the Kruger Park.

The author, publisher and the Kruger Kids Project therefore, assumes no responsibility whatsoever for any experiences occurring to any person as a result of purchasing or reading of this book.

Words To Know

The most important words first

Braai (*bry* - as in fly) — Barbeque, grilling meat over a fire — South Africa's beloved, traditional way of cooking, partying, entertaining, or simply spending time with family and friends.
Boerewors (*boo rah vorce* - as in divorce) — A traditional, spiced sausage, usually grilled on the *braai*.
Wors (*vorce* - as in divorce) — An abbreviation for *boerewors*
Sosatie (*so sarty* - as in party) — A kebab on a skewer, usually grilled on a *braai*.
Pap (*pup* - as in puppy) — Traditional, white maize porridge, usually eaten with *shieba*.
Sheba (*sheba* - as in queen of Sheba) — A cooked sauce consisting of tomatoes and onions.
Rusk — A hard, dried biscuit — similar to a biscotti.

Boerewors on the braai

Sosatie

Pap, sheba and boerewors

Skottel (*scott till*) — A gas-heated wok used to cook bacon, eggs and *boerewors*.
Dop (*dohp*) — Alcohol, or, to drink alcohol
Droëwors (*droo ah vorce* — as in divorce) — Air-dried and spiced *boerewors* - similar to salami.
Biltong (*bill tong*) — Air-dried and spiced meat — similar to American jerky.

Skottel

Droëwors

Biltong

Other words:

Howzit — Abbreviation *for how-is-it*. This is how South Africans greet each other.
Lekker (*lacker*) — Something you say to English or Afrikaans-speaking South Africans to express your approval.
Yebo (*yeah boh*) — Say "yes" to, or acknowledge an African language-speaking South African.
Dumela (*do mell ah*) — "Hello" in the Sotho language.
Sawubona (*suh woo born ah*) — "Hello" in the Zulu language.
Ngiabonga (*nn gee yah bon gah*) — "Thank you" in the Zulu language.
Eish! — The African language version of "Gosh!"
Jislaaik! — (*yis like*) The Afrikaans version of "Gosh!"
Game — Refers to animals in the park, as in "game viewing" — meaning "animal spotting".
Bushveld — Generally refers to any wild eco area in South Africa.

Bundu (boondoo) — A remote part of the bushveld
Lowveld — Generally refers to the north-eastern side of South Africa, including the Kruger National Park.
The Big Five — A most sought after group of large animals to see: elephant, rhino, buffalo, lion, and leopard.
The Small Five — A most sought after group of small creatures to see: elephant shrew, buffalo weaver, leopard tortoise, ant lion, and rhino beetle.

Elephant shrew

Rhino beetle

Leopard tortoise

Drif — A river ford.
Petrol — Gasoline.
Rondavel (*rond ah ville*) — Round thatch-roofed hut accommodation.
Thatch roof — A roof made of dried grass.
Veranda — A porch area in front of a bungalow.
Torch — A flashlight.
Bobbejaan (*bobby yarn*) — Afrikaans for *baboon*.
Aap (*arp* - as in sharp) — Afrikaans for *monkey*.
Kop (corp - without pronouncing the "r") — Afrikaans for a *rocky-outcrop* as in *Pretoriuskop*.
Koppie (*corp ee* - without pronouncing the "r") — A small *kop*.
Boma (*bow mah*) — A reed-enclosed area where a traditional meal is served around a pit-fire.
Lapa (*lah pah*) — Same as *boma*.

Koppie

Boma / lapa

Rondavel

Bakkie (*buckey*) — A utility/pick-up truck.
Bok (as in Ree*bok*) — Afrikaans for any buck/antelope.
Slang (*slung*) — Afrikaans for *snake*.
Leeu (*lew*) — Afrikaans for *lion*.
Spinnekop (*spin a corp*) — Afrikaans for *spider*.
Pad (*putt*) — Afrikaans for *road*.
Grondpad (this is a tough one — you have to start by blowing air across your palette as if you're cleaning it — *ggghh rond putt*) — Afrikaans for *dirt-road*.
Teerpad (*tear-putt*, as in fear) — Afrikaans for *tar-paved road*.
Dam (*dumb*) — Afrikaans for dam/lake, which can also be the English word *dam* with the same meaning.
Vlei (*flay*) — Afrikaans for a river/marsh area.
Pan (*pun*) — An open area where water did or still does accumulate, which is also a potential drinking place for animals.
Padkos (*putt coss*) — The Afrikaans word for *travel food*.

Park Map

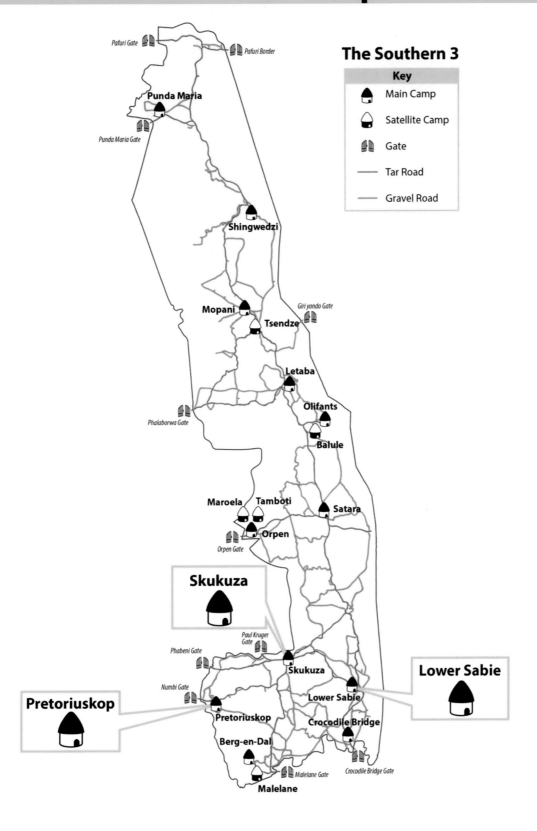

The Southern 3

Key	
🛖	Main Camp
⛺	Satellite Camp
🚪	Gate
—	Tar Road
—	Gravel Road

Pafuri Gate
Pafuri Border

Punda Maria
Punda Maria Gate

Shingwedzi

Mopani
Tsendze
Giri yondo Gate

Letaba

Olifants
Phalaborwa Gate
Balule

Maroela **Tamboti** **Satara**
Orpen
Orpen Gate

Skukuza

Paul Kruger Gate
Phabeni Gate
Skukuza
Numbi Gate
Lower Sabie

Pretoriuskop
Pretoriuskop
Crocodile Bridge
Lower Sabie
Berg-en-Dal
Malelane Gate
Crocodile Bridge Gate
Malelane

General Rest Camp Information

This book is a guide to the southern 3 rest camps of the Kruger Park: Skukuza, Pretoriuskop and Lower Sabie. The purpose of this chapter is to provide general information about all the camps. Each rest camp chapter in this book contains specific information about one of the three camps, and is organised under the same headings as in this *General Information Chapter* for easy reference.

In order to gain the most benefit from this book, read this chapter first before proceeding to the individual camp chapters. Taking note of the general safety precautions, tips and recommendations in this chapter will be helpful as they pertain to all of the others.

View of the Sabie River and railway bridge from Skukuza

Overview:

Rest Camps of the Kruger Park features twelve main rest camps, five small satellite camps, and five bush camps. This book describes the two main camps and one satellite camp in the lower-south part of the park.

The southern 3 main rest camps are Pretoriuskop — located amongst granite koppies — and Skukuza and Lower Sabie — located on the northern bank of the Crocodile River.

All of Kruger's rest camps are magical places. Each one is different and has its own character. However, they all share the same magic. For most, visiting any one as a child usually ignites a passion that burns for a lifetime, resulting in a persistent longing that can only be satisfied by returning to savour the magic again and again.

Each main camp can be described as a small village with most containing a reception, office, shop, petrol station, a la carte restaurant, museum, and a pool. Visitors are accommodated in thatch-roofed bungalows, huts, family cottages, furnished safari tents and guest houses, with campsites also available to campers. Satellite camps usually only offer limited amenities, accommodation units and campsites.

Each camp is fenced and gated to help keep guests and staff safe from animals.

Electric fence around the camp perimeter helps to keep guests and staff safe from animals

The magic of a Kruger Park rest camp begins early in the morning. Just before the sun rises, the sounds of birds begin to drown out the last whooping of the hyenas.

At the same time, Field Guide-accompanied game drive enthusiasts are heard leaving the camp in search of the Big Five, while early unaccompanied game drivers are lined up in their cars waiting for the camp gate to be opened.

Unaccompanied game drivers leave the camp as the gate is opened

Early risers notice the unmistakable smell of the African bush mingling with that of breakfast cooking, bacon and coffee. In some main camps, those who prefer to be catered to are treated to a magnificently prepared breakfast, usually served on an outdoor viewing deck overlooking a river or dam, and the wildlife that have come to drink.

Soon after, the early game drive enthusiasts return to introduce excitement as they share their game sightings and mark them on the sightings board for all to see.

Guests then have choices about how to spend the rest of the day. Some stay in the camp to relax, soak up the atmosphere, sleep, read a book or spend the day on the viewing deck, waiting for wildlife to come to them. Others head out by car to spot game, visit a remote picnic site or bird hide, or to drive to the next camp.

Those who remain in the camp during the day experience a sense of peace and knowing that they are in a very different and special place, unlike any other in the world. Year after year, the atmosphere and activities of the camp are always the same. In contrast, those who go on drives see sights and experience things that are always different, and that can never be reproduced again. By entering the camp and recounting their sightings, their different experiences create the daily camp ritual of storytelling that never changes.

Sitting on a bungalow veranda or a bench under a tree looking out at the African bush, one hears the sound of beetles chaffing their legs, relentless bird calling, and lawn sprinklers splashing water across the hot lawns. The unmistakable aroma of Africa will hang in the air all day before being boosted by the late afternoon smell of bushveld wood, and charcoal burning as the first braai fires are lit.

Each camp has its unique things of interest to visit or explore. Some have a world-class museum that focuses on particular animal species. Others have educational centres that display items of general interest about the park, animals and ancient people who lived in the area thousands of years ago. Skukuza has a museum and well-stocked library that contains an extensive collection of valuable fauna and flora reference and Africana books.

Each camp has a shop, offering traditional foods and drinks, curios, interesting books, safari gear and clothing, and much more. Lovers of varieties of game biltong and South African wines are well-catered to here.

Skukuza Camp shop

The camps are landscaped with interesting indigenous plants and trees. Many of the trees are very mature, and most are name-tagged. Learning to identify them and their features enhances the camp experience by making everything seem more alive.

Guests cannot miss the abundant bird life with their ever-present song that permeates each camp. Water birds can usually be viewed from an observation deck or bird hide which overlooks a dam or river.

Even the smallest camp offers opportunities to walk, exercise, and explore while often stopping to rest and relax on benches facing a perimeter fence, over which one can gaze at the bushveld or hills and mountains beyond.

Skukuza Camp benches overlooking the Sabie River and African bush

As the temperature rises, for some it's time to head for the swimming pool. Each main camp has a swimming pool located in a unique and tranquil setting.

Then it's perhaps time for lunch and drinks on the restaurant deck, admiring the view while the cumulus clouds begin to build all around. By mid-afternoon, there is often lightning and thunder as the summer skies burst open with rain. As quickly as it came, it disappears, allowing the sun to return and shine over the washed camp which then comes alive with insects and a chorus of frogs. As flying ants take to the sky, birds are everywhere to be seen as they, and the frogs on the ground, come to feast. At the same time, excited guests begin to board the Field Guide-accompanied vehicles for night game drives or bush braai dinners.

As sundown approaches, the day game drivers return, and new guests begin to arrive. Now there is activity everywhere as guests take up their accommodations and visit the shop for dinner provisions, while individual fires are being lit in front of most units and campsites.

One of the 2 swimming pools at Skukuza

When the sun sets, the gates are shut for the night. The camp is now alive with the sounds of guests standing around fires, talking, laughing and cooking, while children play and make new friends around the bungalows, tents or caravans. Some families head for the open-air auditorium with their children to watch wildlife movies under the stars. All the while the sound of frogs, bats and owls fill the night, occasionally interrupted by whooping hyenas, hippos and the unmistakable roar of lions.

This is also the time when parents turn up the magic for their children by patrolling the camp fence while flashing torches and searching for reflecting eyes in the dark, on the other side, on the ground and in the trees. This activity almost always produces results and excitement and further ignites their Kruger rest camp passions.

Perimeter bungalow guests and campers are, almost always treated to the sight and sound of whooping hyenas patrolling the fence. Occasionally, they might also see huge buffalo, silent elephants and even lions and leopards that come right up to the fence. Viewing such a spectacle and then also looking up and seeing the splendour of the Milky Way galaxy brightly illuminating the sky above, one is reminded of the privilege of being able to be there to witness it all.

Now the guests who participated in the night game drives or bush braai dinners return and introduce more excitement, as they share their spot-lighted experiences in the bush.

As the evening progresses and the fires begin to die, the accommodation lights begin to go out as those who have plans to rise early retire for the night. Others spend hours on the viewing deck listening to the animal calls and searching for them with their spotlights. Some guests stay up late talking around their campfires. The final magic of the day is the silence that comes over the whole camp towards midnight, which is occasionally broken by hippo grunts, jackal cries and the roar of lions in the distance.

The author, who has religiously returned to experience this for more than 50 years, concludes with the following: *"Each camp is different, but the magic is always the same".*

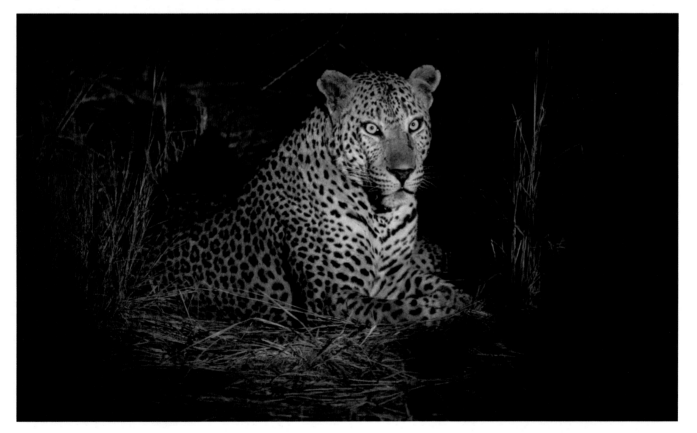

A leopard spotlighted at night

TIP: To make your stay enjoyable in any camp, remember to pack in the items below before leaving home:

- Warm jacket
- Tracksuit/sweater
- Head warmer
- Basic first-aid kit
- Camera
- Binoculars
- Sun hat
- Swimming towels
- Wash basin plug
- Mosquito repellant
- Headlamp, torch and spotlight
- If visiting with a baby, a fold-up camp cot

Additional items are also listed in this chapter for self-catering, birding, game viewing, and tree-spotting.

TIP: Pack lightly. Regularly dragging big suitcases in and out of cars is not fun. Accommodation unit interiors are also often small, and cupboard space is limited. The convenience of camp laundromats allow you to clean your clothes, so there is no need to over-pack.

Travel routes:

The rest camps of the southern Kruger area can be accessed via multiple gates. This makes it possible to reach the camps conveniently from Mozambique in the east, Swaziland and KwaZulu-Natal in the south, and Mpumalanga in the southwest and west.

The closest cities and towns are Mbombela/Nelspruit and White River in the southwest and Malelane and Komatipoort in the south. If narrow, pot-holed roads, human and animal traffic or possible roadside crime is a concern, then the most popular, as well as generally the safest route to reach all of the southern rest camps is via the N4 freeway and the Malelane gate.

Travel distances and times to the camps from towns and cities are referenced in each camp chapter of this book.

Crocodile Bridge Gate

The approximate distances to the southern park gates are as shown below:

Gate	Johannesburg	Maputo	Durban	Cape Town	Bloemfontein
Numbi	392 KM	242 KM	794 KM	1,846 KM	793 KM
Malelane	407 KM	144 KM	784 KM	1,812 KM	812 KM
Phabeni	417 KM	276 KM	817 KM	1,817 KM	817 KM
Crocodile Bridge	455 KM	111 KM	832 KM	1,854 KM	854 KM
Paul Kruger	447 KM	300 KM	847 KM	1,846 KM	846 KM

CAUTION: Driving to the park at night is not advisable as it can be dangerous, especially if your car breaks down.

The Paul Kruger Memorial at the Paul Kruger Gate

Nearest airports:

Oliver Tambo airport in Johannesburg and Maputo airport in Mozambique are the closest international airports to the southern camps of the park. However, connecting flights land not only at Mpumalanga Kruger Airport which is 40 KM from the nearest gate, but also right inside the park at Skukuza Airport.

Travel distances and times from airports to the camps are included in each camp chapter of this book.

Skukuza Airport

Skukuza Airport entrance statue

Camp gate open and close times:

Travellers to the park and camps should always consider the camp and park gate opening and closing times when planning their journeys:

Park gate times	Jan	Feb	Mar	Apr	May	Jun	Jul	Aug	Sep	Oct	Nov	Dec
5:30 am – 6.30 pm	•	•									•	•
5:30 am – 6.00 pm			•							•		
6:00 am – 6.00 pm				•				•	•			
6:00 am – 5.30 pm					•	•	•					

Camp gate times	Jan	Feb	Mar	Apr	May	Jun	Jul	Aug	Sep	Oct	Nov	Dec
4:30 am – 6.30 pm	•										•	•
5:30 am – 6.30 pm		•										
5:30 am – 6.00 pm			•							•		
6:00 am – 6.00 pm				•				•	•			
6:00 am – 5.30 pm					•	•	•					

Climate:

The rest camps in the southern part of Kruger experience comfortable subtropical temperatures throughout the year. Thatched roofs provide a natural cooling effect in most accommodations for most of the year, while air-conditioning comes to the rescue during the height of summer which can become uncomfortably hot. Summer also brings wonderful thunderstorms, although it can also cause flooding as well as a muddy mess for campers.

The clear skies, cooler days and chilly evenings make rainless winters the most comfortable time of the year to visit the rest camps in the southern part of the Kruger Park. High and low temperatures and precipitation data have been provided in this book for each camp.

Amenities and services overview:

Depending on upon the camp size, each offers a range of amenities, services and activities provided by friendly and courteous staff members. Field Guides and restaurant staff are usually up before sunrise while others work late into the night to ensure that guests have memorable experiences. Others serve in the shop, clean and service accommodations, show movies at night, and provide educational programmes, limited road services and first-aid.

Most camps offer the following amenities and services:

- **Check-in, reception and info centre:**

Usually located close to the entrance, overnight visitors must stop here to check in on arrival. They are given a camp map and shown how to reach the accommodation unit that has been allocated to them. Efficient reception staff members are also available to change reservations. This can include them accessing the computerised booking system or calling other camps to inquire about alternatives. At the same time at an adjoining desk, visitors can book game drives and walks, bush braai dinners, report possible problems, and get travel information. At Skukuza, the reception centre also includes a car-hire desk, post office and bank. Reception office hours are:

Times	Jan	Feb	Mar	Apr	May	Jun	Jul	Aug	Sep	Oct	Nov	Dec
7.30 am – 6.00 pm					•	•	•					
7.30 am – 6.30 pm			•	•				•	•	•		
7.30 am – 7.00 pm	•	•									•	•

The office phone numbers, name and email address of the duty manager for each camp are provided in each camp chapter of this book.

• Wildlife-viewing decks:

Some camps, like Skukuza and Lower Sabie, have large viewing decks that overlook bodies of water and the wildlife that come to drink. Guests can sit and view the panorama from benches. Those who prefer air-conditioned, mosquito-free interiors on hot summer days can enjoy the view through the large restaurant windows. Many prefer to spend the whole day here waiting for the wildlife to come to them instead of searching for them by car.

Wildlife-viewing decks at Skukuza

• Field Guide-accompanied walks:

Kruger Park guided game walks provide one of life's unique opportunities to see what the world looked like before the advent of modern human civilisation. Everything that you see, smell, hear, touch and feel while walking is what the prehistoric people of the area experienced thousands of years ago. Where else in the world would you be able to do this while being protected from animals that would potentially put your life in danger if it weren't for the two experienced and armed Field Guides who accompany and protect you? It is one of those experiences that must be regarded as priceless, yet it can be experienced from any main rest camp in the Kruger National Park, often for the price of a meal at a restaurant.

You are transported from the camp, either at dawn or late afternoon and dropped off in a remote part of the bush, where you walk for 1-3 hours with a small group and your guides.

The armed Field Guides are knowledgeable professionals. Along the way you are occasionally stopped to be educated about the plants, trees, animals and their spoor. You can also quietly stand and resonate with the unspoiled ambience of the bushveld. The walks are not strenuous hikes. They are taken at a leisurely pace with plenty of stops along the way. Unfortunately, children under the age of 12, and adults older than 65 are not allowed to participate (adults over 65 can participate if they have a doctor's certificate of fitness).

You will be expected to dress in neutral colours, like khaki, which will blend in with the surroundings. To avoid animal detection, you are expected not to apply deodorant or perfume. Also, while walking, you should try to speak as little and as softly as possible. Finally, you should be armed with a good camera and be prepared to take photographs to record lifelong memories of an experience, never to be forgotten.

TIP: All are recommended to visit the toilet before leaving.

TIP: Use a small backpack to carry water and a few snacks to eat along the way.

TIP: Wear comfortable walking shoes.

TIP: Wear long sleeve shirts and long pants that will protect you from ticks, mosquitoes and the sun.

TIP: This activity is definitely more enjoyable during winter months when temperatures are cooler.

CAUTION: Be aware that walking in the wild is dangerous. Anything can happen along the way, and the animals do not know that tourists are off the menu. So, go with open eyes, follow your guide's instructions carefully and stay alert at all times. If you are not fit or unable to run from danger or climb a tree if required, then you might want to reconsider this camp-provided activity.

Field Guide-accompanied walkers

• Open-vehicle game drives:

There was a time when the exciting experience of hiring an open-top, off-road vehicle and being driven into remote areas of the bush by an experienced Field Guide was the exclusive domain of the luxury private game reserves bordering the park. Now these adrenalin-pumping activities are also generally available to main rest camp guests.

Each camp offers three or more game drives per day. One leaves early in the morning before sunrise, a second leaves in the late afternoon and a third leaves at night. Small groups are taken in 6-8-seater vehicles, and large groups of up to 21 are taken in specially-fitted open trucks. These game drives last for 2-4 hours and usually follow the public tar and dirt roads. Physically challenged guests can participate, but may need to be lifted into the vehicle by others.

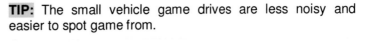

TIP: The small vehicle game drives are less noisy and easier to spot game from.

At a higher cost, small groups can also hire an off-road vehicle and Field Guide. This opportunity is only offered at some camps, but is available for a whole-day excursion to explore areas that are off-limits to the public. To avoid disappointment, one should book a few months in advance.

Unfortunately, children under six years of age are not allowed.

TIP: For all drives, take your own food and drink and don't forget your camera and binoculars.

TIP: For day drives, take sunscreen, a hat, and a long sleeve shirt.

For night drives, take mosquito repellant, something to keep your head and legs warm, a jacket and gloves, and don't forget your torch or better still, your own spotlight.

TIP: All are advised to visit the toilet before leaving on the drive.

TIP: A small seat cushion makes the trip much more comfortable after the first hour.

NOTE: The game drive image shown above shows a vehicle being used by a private safari company. The game drive vehicles used by SANParks tend to be more closed-in to provide guests with more shade, comfort and protection from animals.

Game drive vehicle used by all Kruger Park Field Guides for small groups

21-seater Game drive vehicle used by all Kruger Park Field Guides for large groups

CAUTION: Be aware that driving up to wild animals with an open-top vehicle can be dangerous. Anything can happen. So, follow your Field Guide or driver's instructions and stay alert at all times. Keep still and don't stand up or climb off the vehicle unless you have been given permission to do so.

• Laundromats:

Every camp has one or more laundry and ironing rooms that have been fitted with automatic washers and dryers that operate with R2 and R5 coins.

TIP: Pack a supply of R2 and R5 coins before leaving home as they are hard to come by in some of the camps. An exception is Skukuza which has a mini bank in the reception and information centre.

TIP: Bring your own wash basin plug, detergent, softener, pot scourer and iron.

• Petrol station and car wash:

Each main rest camp has a petrol station. A car wash and vacuuming service is offered next to the petrol station of most main rest camps. There are no automated car washes. Instead, expect to receive a very good hand-wash from a friendly worker.

TIP: Come prepared, with a folding camp-chair and a book, or something to occupy your time when heading to the car wash.

TIP: Bring cash. Some of the petrol stations and all of the car washes do not accept credit cards.

- ## Emergency road service:

Some camps offer limited emergency road services, usually only providing that which is needed to get a visitor's broken-down vehicle back to safety. Travellers who are stranded can call 0800 030 666 to summon help from the nearest camp that offers service. Skukuza offers a limited repair service.

- ## Communal Kitchens:

Each camp offers communal kitchens to guests who are either camping or staying in accommodations that do not have kitchens. They are conveniently located in the campsite or behind huts and bungalows. Each is equipped with running hot water and sinks for dish washing, hot plates for cooking and urns of water that are kept boiling 24 hours a day.

There are also food preparation areas and ample electric plugs for those who have brought their favourite kitchen gadgets from home. Some are also fitted with a stove and oven, a deep freeze and cupboards for storage. Communal kitchens are great places to swop game drive successes and make new friends.

Communal kitchen at Pretoriuskop Camp

- ## Crockery and Cutlery Hampers:

To compliment these facilities, crockery and cutlery hampers are also made available for hire to guests. Each hamper consists of the basics to prepare and eat a meal for two.

TIP: Bring a wash basin plug, dishwashing liquid, pot scourer and dish cloths.

- ## First-aid assistance:

Certain camp staff members are trained to provide assistance to guests who experience minor scrapes and accidents. For more urgent medical problems, Skukuza Camp has a resident doctor for guests to consult. Guests who are in need should immediately report to the camp reception and information centre.

- ## Accommodation servicing:

All camp accommodation units, including safari tents, are serviced every day by the camp hospitality staff. Included are the cleaning of bathrooms, bedrooms and kitchens, as well as the changing of bed linen. Fresh towels and soap are also provided. Verandas and outdoor areas are swept, and braai grills are cleaned. Servicing is carried out after guests have vacated their accommodation in the mornings until 2.00 pm. On arrival, guests will always find clean and tidy accommodation units awaiting them.

All camp accommodation units, including verandas, kitchens and outdoor areas are swept and cleaned daily.

- ## Cable television:

There are no televisions in the bungalows, huts, guest cottages or safari tents in any of the camps. However, the guest houses in the main camps all have cable television, as well as the restaurant lounge areas and separate communal TV rooms. Not to spoil the atmosphere that guests have travelled to the Kruger Park to experience, the restaurant TVs are limited in number and not loud and intrusive, usually providing sports coverage only. After all, even the most fanatical Kruger Park guest is not going to appreciate missing a South African Springboks vs. New Zealand All Blacks rugby match.

- ## Cell phone reception:

Until recently, all of the camps had pay telephones. However, due to the advent of cellular phones, they have all been removed. Cell phone coverage is now available in all main camps and most satellite camps.

- ## ATM:

Some of the main camps have ATMs. Check the individual camp chapters to confirm. These remote ATMs have limited funds and guests should be cautious about expecting to withdraw large amounts of cash. Users can also expect to be charged additional fees when withdrawing money.

CAUTION: The electricity supply to camps can be unreliable at times. In such an event, the ATMs don't work. Therefore, be prepared by bringing cash.

- ## Communal ablution facilities:

Each camp offers communal bathrooms to guests who are either camping or staying in accommodations that do not have private bathrooms or toilets. They are conveniently located in the campsite or behind huts and bungalows. Each is equipped with running hot water, sinks, showers and a bath. These facilities are serviced every day and are usually clean and in good working order.

TIP: The best time to use the communal ablution facilities is around 8.00 am, right after they have been serviced and most guests have left the camp for the day. Another good time is about 3.30 pm, just before the evening rush.

TIP: Flip-flops or Crocs are a good idea when using the communal showers.

TIP: Some communal ablutions have limited hooks for hanging your items. Therefore, either take only a few items into them or take your own over-the-shower-door hooks.

Communal ablution building at Pretoriuskop Camp

- ## Internet coverage and Wi-Fi:

South African residents, who have contracted one or more of the wireless internet providers like MTN or Vodacom, are usually lucky enough to pick up internet coverage in the main rest camps.

International visitors on the other hand usually resort to buying airtime or data which can be accessed via a mobile router or similar device. Unfortunately, these systems are hopelessly unreliable as of 2016, and in the author's opinion, not worth the money.

- ## Postbox:

Every main rest camp has a post box, usually located in front of the reception or shop. For camps that don't have a post box, guests can drop mail off at the reception to be forwarded to a camp that does have one.

Power points for caravan campers:

All of the main rest camp campsites and most of their satellite camps provide power to campers. Check the individual camp chapters to confirm. However, the power points are grouped together and users often need their own long extension cords to reach them as well as the popular camper's blue connector.

See more information and tips for campers under the *Campsites* heading below.

• **Outdoor wildlife movies in the evenings:**

Most camps show wildlife documentary movies, usually in an outdoor auditorium. Of only 30 – 60 minutes duration, this is a tradition that has survived and added more than 50 years of evening camp magic to guests. There is something very special about sitting under the star-filled night sky with a crowd of excited kids learning about the animals that one might encounter the next day. Even for those not watching, the familiar nightly sound of the narrator adds to the camp atmosphere.

TIP: Bring a warm jacket during winter months and mosquito repellant during the summer months. Snacks or a flask of hot tea or coffee adds to the fun.

Lower Sabie outdoor auditorium for wildlife movies at night

• **Children's educational programmes:**

The Kruger National Park offers programmes to educate children about the park including its fauna and flora, economic and social benefits to the country and surrounding communities, as well as the importance of supporting efforts to combat poaching. Daily programmes are available, as well those that require overnight accommodation. Skukuza camp offers a dormitory to accommodate large groups of children as well as their adult chaperones.

Accommodation for groups of children

Educational programme children returning from game drive

- ## Auditorium and conference facilities:

Some of the main camps offer very well-equipped conference facilities for small or large groups. Attendees have the advantage of overnight accommodation, restaurant or self-catering meals as well as camp-provided game drives and other team-building activities.

Skukuza Camp conference centre

Restaurant:

Most camps offer their guests a restaurant, coffee and take away foods snack bar. From a world-class buffet-style breakfast at Skukuza's Cattle Baron restaurant, to the gourmet a la carte delights of the *Mugg & Bean* at Lower Sabie, to the legendary burgers and coffee at the Pretoriuskop Wimpy, there is plenty to delight local and international guests alike.

The restaurant deck at Lower Sabie Camp

Restaurant deck at Skukuza Camp

For a more intimate experience, diners at some of the camps can enjoy a boma braai, a traditional meal served around a pit fire in a reed-enclosed area.

For extreme African atmosphere-dining seekers, there is also the opportunity to experience fully catered bush braais outside the camp. Diners are transported in the early evening to a remote location where a fire and candlelit dining table has been prepared for them. While listening to the calls of animals, a five-course gourmet meal is enjoyed under the protective watch of park rangers. The evening is then finished off with a spotlighted night game drive back to the camp. Both the boma braai and the bush braai have to be pre-booked with the camp reception.

Shop:

Every main camp has a shop that offers guests everything that they need to make their visit more enjoyable. Included in most camp shops is a range of frozen and packaged foods as well as an impressive display of dried fruits and every kind of game biltong and boerewors imaginable. Fresh fruit and vegetables are also available, but are more limited.

The fridges are filled with fruit juices, cool drinks and beers, and there is usually a good selection of South African wines to choose from on the shelves. Campers and self-caterers alike will find that *one* thing that they forgot to pack in, as well as charcoal, bushveld firewood, starters and even instant braai boxes.

All kinds of books and videos about the park, animals, trees and birds are also available, as well as maps and reference guides. Camera accessories, binoculars and torches for game and bird-watchers are on sale, as well as safari clothing gear to make them look the part.

Sweets, ice cream and traditional treats like koeksisters and milk tarts — as well as patent medicines for those who have over-indulged — complete the list. Friendly, courteous and helpful staff wrap up the enjoyable experience of visiting a rest camp shop.

Skukuza Camp shop

TIP: As previously mentioned, **bring cash**. The electricity supply in the camps is not always reliable. When it goes off, credit cards are useless, making it impossible to pay for shop or restaurant purchases.

Camp birds:

Bird-lovers can spend days wandering around, spotting and photographing the enormous variety of species that can be seen in the trees, and wading in rivers or dams which are in sight of most camps. Some even have secluded hides overlooking drinking holes and pans. Their walls are adorned with labelled bird pictures, making it possible for beginners to leave with the gift of identifying a host of birds. Silence is required, and also often rewarded, by game that quietly approach to drink.

Lake Panic Bird Hide at Skukuza

TIP: For enjoyable birding, remember to pack in the items listed below, before leaving home:

- Bird field guide
- Camera
- Binoculars

- Sunglasses
- Pen
- Note book

- Sunscreen
- Digital audio recorder
- Sun hat

Camp trees:

Most of the trees in the camps are name-tagged, making it possible to spend as much time as one wants to learn their names and features. Some camps provide background information and stories about the origins of the tree names, their value to the fauna and flora, and their medicinal benefits for humans. Taking the time to learn about the trees and touching and photographing their seeds, leaves, fruit and flowers, enhances one's visit to the park with a whole new perspective, making everything seem more alive.

A tagged bushveld gardenia tree at Pretoriuskop

TIP: For the best tree identification experience, remember to pack in the items listed below, before leaving home:

- Tree field guide
- Camera

- Binoculars
- Sunglasses

- Sun hat
- Sunscreen

Day visitors' picnic site:

In the past, day visitors were allowed to picnic inside the rest camps. This caused overcrowding and noise which spoiled the experience for overnight-guests. This problem was solved by creating comfortable day visitor picnic sites adjoining or separate from some of the camps. Most have all of the amenities necessary to negate the need for day visitors to picnic in the camp, such as a snack shop, skottel rentals, ablutions, shady picnic sites, benches, tables and chairs, and even a swimming pool, lawns and a playground for kids.

Unlike the park picnic sites that are not associated with camps, these sites are fenced to protect the visitors from dangerous animals. However, some of the separate picnic sites like at Pretoriuskop do not yet have all the amenities described and see very few visitors or even have staff in attendance. Non-picnicking day visitors to the camps can visit the shop, restaurant and game viewing deck, which is part of the main building and accessible to the public.

TIP: Remember to pack the below items in before heading for a picnic site:

- Picnic hamper including crockery and cutlery
- Paper serviettes and towels
- Corkscrew and bottle opener
- Zip-lock plastic bags for leftovers and dry foods
- Food, spices, sauces and drinks (no alcohol)
- Matches or lighter
- Table cloth with clips to stop blowing away
- Braai tongs
- Oven gloves to adjust a hot braai grill
- Braai grill brush
- Charcoal

- Fire starters
- Tin foil
- Folding chairs
- Swimming towels
- Camera
- Binoculars
- Sunglasses
- Sun hat
- Sunscreen
- Mosquito repellant
- Cash

Skukuza day visitors' centre swimming pool

Things to do:

Each camp chapter in this book describes the various activities that guests can partake in. Some activities have been included above under the *Amenities and Services* heading while others are described below.

In-camp suggested walks:

As previously mentioned, even the smallest camp offers opportunities to walk. Walking in the camps not only provides good exercise and a break from the many hours spent game viewing in a car, but it also provides a different perspective to a camp visit.

Along the way are many interesting things to see including birds, trees and flowers to become acquainted with. It's also a great way to explore and seek out that perfect bungalow or campsite for the next visit.

Guests have a choice of walking along the paved roadways and lawns, the perimeter fence pathways, or a combination of both.

The author has spent much time walking in the camps and has included his suggested routes in the individual camp chapter overview maps, a description, and the following data for each:

- Distance
- Climb gradient
- Surface
- Shade
- Benches
- Toilet availability
- Views
- Opportunities to view game

Author suggested walking route shown in camp overview maps

Finally, a camp walk is a wonderful way to make new friends along the way.

Riverside walkway at Skukuza Camp

CAUTION: Always use a torch when walking at night, so that you can look out for snakes and small nocturnal animals which you might not want to bump into.

CAUTION: The electric wires above the perimeter fences actually *do* work — Do not test them!

Swimming pool:

During summer, the heat can become quite oppressive, which ushers in an opportunity to head for the camp swimming pool. Once again, each camp's pool is in a unique setting and usually surrounded by lawns under shady trees, often with playground equipment for small children. These are perfect retreats from the heat for families and picnickers who are vigilant enough to watch out for monkeys that are always ready to run up and steal a snack or two.

TIP: Remember to pack your swimming gear in before leaving home.

Pretoriuskop Camp Swimming Pool

Camp animals:

Animals and birds that live in some of the camps include warthogs, bushbuck, squirrels, tortoises, monitor lizards, blue-headed agamas, and guinea fowl. These animals, although not tame, have become accustomed to human activity.

Vervet monkey

Monitor lizards are often in the rest camps

Wild animals that enter the camps during the day include vervet monkeys, baboons, and snakes. During the night, guests might also come across bush babies, civets, genets, rats, bats, various mongooses, frogs, and owls.

CAUTION: Never feed any of the animals inside or outside the rest camps. Doing so only encourages them to associate humans with food, which over time the animals become increasingly aggressive about claiming, resulting in them ultimately having to be put down.

CAUTION: Some camps have areas that have been left natural. Keep children out of these areas to avoid encountering ticks, snakes, and spiders in the long grass.

CAUTION: Monkeys and baboons are frequent visitors to all rest camps (baboons are less frequent).

To avoid potential problems with these animals, keep your car windows, tent flaps and accommodation doors closed at all times and don't leave any food in sight, especially unattended.

Be particularly vigilant when arriving at your accommodation or campsite, as they will help to unpack your car if you leave an open boot or door unattended.

Do not leave items lying around in brown paper bags or plastic containers as monkeys associate them with food. Neglecting this tip could result in you seeing that special souvenir that you bought at the shop being examined by small hands and eyes in the tree branches above you.

CAUTION: Be cautious when entering ablution blocks, especially at night. Monkeys, baboons and snakes sometimes enter for warmth or to find food or shelter.

CAUTION: Be on the look-out for snakes that will enter the camp if the surrounding veld has recently or is currently experiencing fire.

Skukuza Camp warthogs

Game viewing from the camp:

The camps are protected from animals by a high perimeter fence. On the inside of the fence is the camp with its accommodation and communal structures, amenities and people. On the outside is the African wild.

To view the animals, there are viewing decks, bird hides and perimeter trails with benches to sit on and wait for the animals to come and go. Many perimeter accommodation units look right at or over the perimeter fence, making it possible to spend the whole day game viewing from a veranda.

During the day and with a little luck on one's side, any animal can be seen from all of the camps. Some come right up to the fence, and sometimes elephants even extend their trunks over as they reach for their favourite leaves on camp trees.

Camps that overlook bodies of water offer the most opportunities for game viewing from the camp.

TIP: Remember to pack in the game viewing items listed below before leaving home:

- Animal field guide
- Camera
- Binoculars
- Sunglasses
- Sun hat
- Sunscreen

Elephants at the perimeter fence

Game viewing from the camp at night:

All of the camps come alive at night with the clinking sounds of fruit bats, the chirping of crickets, the calls of owls and the croaking of frogs, all blended with the occasional whooping and cackling of hyenas, screeching of jackals, grunting of hippos, and the unmistakable roars from the king of the jungle.

Shining a light through or over the fence to spot eyes reflecting back or animals nearby is lots of fun, especially for kids. This activity is most productive in front of perimeter accommodations or the campgrounds, where hyenas are

almost always seen patrolling the fence. Sometimes, remaining still and with lights off until rustling is heard, you can catch civets or wild cats in your torchlight as they forage near the fence.

Other animals that could be spotted over the fence include bush babies, polecats, caracals, honey badgers, and springhares.

For some, game viewing from the camp at night is a highlight. Shining a light into the bushveld can produce the most unexpected surprises all wrapped up in the wonderful atmosphere created by the sight and smell of cooking fires, sounds of nocturnal animals, birds, frogs, insects, bats, the bright stars, dark shadows and the outline of trees all around.

CAUTION: Always remember not to shine a light directly into an animal's eyes as this can damage them. Instead, shine your light at the body of the animal, avoiding the eyes.

CAUTION: Never throw food over the fence as that will ultimately lead to animals having to be put down when they associate humans with food.

CAUTION: Do not patrol remote parts of the perimeter fence at night and stay away from external trees that overhang the fence.

TIP: Remember to pack in the night game viewing items listed below before leaving home:

- Animal and reptile field guide
- A strong flashlight and torch

- Camera
- Binoculars

- Mosquito repellant
- A warm jacket

As night falls, it's time to take out torches and spotlights and to start game viewing from the camp.

Accommodation overview:

Kruger Park Rest Camp guests have a number of accommodation options. The first consideration when choosing is the number of people in your party and who wants to stay together. Some units only accommodate 2-3 people while others are available to groups of 10 people or more. The next consideration is price, which is usually dictated by 1) whether the unit has a view of a perimeter fence or of a body of water such as a dam or river, and 2) whether the unit includes private cooking, bathroom and toilet facilities or if it shares communal facilities.

Guests can apply the above needs and choices to any of the below-listed types of accommodation.

TIP: While meat and other foodstuffs to cook can be bought at any camp shop, self-catering accommodation units usually include whatever one needs to prepare and consume meals. However, there are a few items that guests should bring from home to ensure that any items that have gone missing or are not included do not spoil their stay. Below are some good suggestions:

- Paper serviettes and towels
- Corkscrew and bottle opener
- Zip-lock plastic bags for leftovers and dry foods
- Vegetable peeler and utility knife
- Braai tongs
- Plastic salad bowl
- Jug
- Oven gloves to adjust a hot braai grill
- Braai grill brush
- Steak knives
- Headlamp
- Tin foil
- Basting brush

Campsites:

Camping is the least expensive accommodation option. Up to 6 people per stand can stay in tents or caravans. Although stands with perimeter or water views, shade or those closest to the communal facilities are the most sought after, the rate to occupy them is the same as any other.

Very seldom are the actual stands demarcated, and getting one that appeals to you usually requires getting there early in the morning when some of the previous night's campers are packing up to leave. During the holiday seasons, the main rest camp campsites can become quite crowded which has positives and negatives. Those that enjoy interacting with other guests and the resulting communal atmosphere experience the crowds positively. Those that prefer a more solitary experience should either visit out of holiday season or choose the smaller and quieter satellite campsites.

Most camp site stands are on flat ground and include a free-standing braai grill. A limited number also include a picnic table with built-in seats. Electricity is available to most via plug points that are usually grouped together as opposed to being located per site.

Camping is more enjoyable during the cooler months. It is not very comfortable during the height of summer unless a very shaded site is selected or one is camping in an air-conditioned caravan or camper.

All of the campsites include one or more communal ablution, kitchen and laundry buildings and most have at least one that is accessible to guests in wheelchairs.

Camping is an especially wonderful option for families with children who enjoy making and playing with new friends.

TIP: The braai grills are not fixed in many of the campsites, and there are sometimes not enough for every stand. Get there early, claim a grill that suits your needs best and set it up on your stand.

CAUTION: Baboons and monkeys know how to operate zips to get inside tents to steal food. Pack in 10 cm lengths' of domestic wire or small padlocks to secure your tent zips when away from your stand.

CAUTION: Be on the look-out for spiders and scorpions that might creep into shoes and nooks, crannies and between blankets inside tents.

TIP: Campers should bring long extension cords with them and also make sure they include the standard blue electrical plug or an SA 3 pin plug adapter to connect.

TIP: Campsite communal ablutions do not provide towels. Remember to bring your own.

TIP: Campsites don't always include tables and seats. Always bring a folding table and chairs with you.

Skukuza Camp Site

Safari tents:

One of the most economical accommodation options is to stay in a safari tent. Unlike what usually comes to mind when thinking of tenting, the safari tents are fully furnished and serviced daily.

Accommodating up to 4 guests, each tent includes single beds with bedding, a fridge, cupboard, electricity, a ceiling fan, screened windows and doors, veranda or patio table and chairs, a lock-up pantry and a fixed braai grill. Luxury safari tents also include kitchenettes, a wash basin, toilet and shower. Communal bathrooms and kitchens are located close to safari tents that do not have their own, and picnic hampers that include cutlery and crockery are available for rent from reception.

TIP: Safari tents don't seal perfectly, and it's therefore not impossible for unwanted insects to enter. Shining a fluorescent light on the floor will turn a scorpion fluorescent so that you see and do not step on one. So, pack one in before leaving home.

CAUTION: Unlike nearly all huts and bungalows, safari tents are not air-conditioned. Staying in one is, therefore, most enjoyable during the cooler winter months and not very comfortable during the height of summer.

CAUTION: When booked into a safari tent, arrive early enough to inspect for holes and tears and possibly request to be moved if any are found. This will ensure that whatever made a hole does not become an uninvited guest.

CAUTION: To deter thieving monkeys and baboons, lock all of your food away in the secure pantry cage that is provided with each tent. Alternatively you can lock your non-perishable foods in your car boot.

TIP: To discourage monkeys and baboons from trying to steal food from you, visit a novelty store and buy a rubber snake before leaving home. Left in sight of primates, this sometimes frightens them away. This trick has also been known to work with a picture of a leopard's face.

Furnished Safari Tent at Lower Sabie Camp

Huts:

Dating back to the 1930s, round-walled huts with thatched roofs are the traditional type of accommodation in the park. Initially, these units, also known as *rondavels*, had no windows, wash basin, toilet, kitchenette or veranda and were ventilated via a small space between the top of the walls and the roof. A very small number of these huts still remain in the northern park while the rest have all been upgraded to include some or all of the above features and more. Most units are free-standing while some are attached to each other.

Huts usually accommodate 1-3 people in single beds while a few also include bunk beds to sleep up to 6 people. Communal bathrooms and kitchens are located close to huts that do not have their own and picnic hampers that include cutlery and crockery are available for rent from reception.

They are economically priced, the 2-sleeper Pretoriuskop huts being the best value-for-money units in the southern park. Huts are also a good option for any season because they are all air-conditioned.

Readers should check the tables provided in the individual camp chapters to see what is included in the different huts. However, before making reservations one should always double-check because upgrading of the huts is ongoing.

2-sleeper huts at Pretoriuskop Camp

Bungalows:

Usually accommodating up to 4 people, bungalows are an upgrade to huts. Some are configured with more than one room and nearly all are free-standing. While most are constructed in the traditional round rondavel with thatched-roof style, some are clustered, like at Lower Sabie and Pretoriuskop, or duplexes like at Skukuza.

Bungalows almost always include a wash basin, toilet, shower or bath, kitchenette and veranda with outdoor furniture and a braai grill. Kitchenettes include cooking pots, a frying pan, crockery and cutlery for four people, a bread knife, egg lifter, tin and bottle openers, and a water jug.

Duplex bungalows at Skukuza Camp

Family cottages:

Family cottages are similar to non-rondavel style bungalows that can accommodate up to 6 people. All include two or more room configurations with small kitchens and two bathrooms, one being en-suite.

Family cottage at Pretoriuskop Camp

Guest houses:

To accommodate large groups, each main camp offers 1-3 private guest houses. They all have multiple rooms, en-suite and separate bathrooms, a lounge, pub, full kitchen, cable television, expansive verandas and shaded parking. Some houses consist of a communal house with small detached rooms.

Each house is privately positioned and screened from the rest of the camp and usually located for spectacular views of a river, dam or bushveld vista. Game viewing is almost always guaranteed from an expansive veranda or large outdoor-cooking and entertaining area.

Guest House at Skukuza Camp

Skukuza

View of the Sabie River from Skukuza

Overview:

Skukuza is the biggest and busiest camp in the park. It is located in the south-western part of the park, bounded by the Sabie Sand private game reserve to the north, overlooking the Kruger Park's only perennial river, the mighty Sabie. It lies in an ecological area called the *Sabie/Crocodile Thorn Thickets*.

Skukuza is like a mini-town and is the most visited of all the camps. It houses the administrative headquarters of the park, plus the famous Stevenson Library and Museum. Other amenities include a large shop, restaurant and cafeteria, large conference facilities, a nursery, church, golf course, airport, car hire and other commercial conveniences for visitors.

Skukuza offers visitors a wide range of accommodations, including guest houses, family cottages, round rondavel-style bungalows and huts, as well as campsites with ablution and cooking facilities.

Visitors love Skukuza because of the aura of excitement and interest that it generates, particularly for arriving visitors before they embark on their less-commercial journeys into the rest of the park.

This camp's popularity is also due to it being part of the most game-saturated area of the park. It is surrounded by multiple good roads leading to popular waterholes, hides and lookout points that make Big Five game viewing very rewarding.

A full range of family friendly activities, game drives, hikes, bush meals, and amenities such as two pools and a viewing deck also contribute to making this camp one of the park's top favourites.

The only downsides to Skukuza are its unending busyness, relative noise and commercial activities that detract from a bushveld experience, and also comparatively high river-view accommodation costs.

With exciting views of the Sabie River, expansive lawns and shaded picnic areas, Skukuza offers an exciting first stop for those arriving, or a last opportunity to stock up on curios and souvenirs for those saying their goodbyes to the park.

GPS co-ordinates:

S 24 59' 43   E 31 35' 34"

Travel routes:

Route 1. From Johannesburg via White River: Take the N4 freeway to Nelspruit/Mbombela, to White River, to Numbi Gate and then on to Skukuza.

Route 2. From Johannesburg via Malelane: Take the N4 freeway to Nelspruit/Mbombela, to Malelane, to Malelane Gate and then on to Skukuza.

Route 3: From Maputo via Malelane: Take the EN4 freeway to the Mozambique border, to the N4 to Malelane, to Malelane Gate and then on to Skukuza.

From	KM to gate	Drive time to gate	Park Gate	KM from gate	Drive time from gate	Route
Johannesburg via White River	391	4.25 hours	Numbi	55	1.50 hours	1
Johannesburg via Malelane	405	4.25 hours	Malelane	63	1.75 hours	2
Maputo via Malelane	146	2 hours	Malelane	63	1.75 hours	3

Nearest airports:

Airport	KM	Drive time	Via gate
Oliver Tambo Int. Airport Johannesburg (JNB, FAJS)	485	5.50 hours	Malelane
Oliver Tambo Int. Airport Johannesburg (JNB, FAJS)	431	5.50 hours	Numbi
Mpumalanga Int. Airport in White River (MQP, FAKN)	113	1.75 hours	Paul Kruger
Skukuza Airport in the Kruger Park (SZK, FASZ)	5	10 minutes	-
Maputo Int. Airport in Mozambique (MPM)	191	4 hours	Crocodile Bridge
Mpumalanga Int. Airport in White River (MQP, FAKN)	105	2.25 hours	Numbi
East Gate Airport in Hoedspruit (HDS)	152	2.75 hours	Paul Kruger
Polokwane Int. Airport (PTG, FAPP)	354	4.50 hours	Paul Kruger

CAUTION: Please note that all travel times quoted are approximate and are dependent on weather, time of day, game-viewer cars blocking the road, and other unforeseen circumstances.

Check-in: &

Overnight visitors must check in at reception, which is immediately to the left when driving into the camp. The office phone number is 013 735 4196. The Duty Manager is Mari Morland who can also be reached by email at mari.morland@sanparks.org.

Climate:

Skukuza enjoys pleasant weather all year round. Winters are sunny and warm to mild with temperatures ranging from 7-26 degrees Celsius. Nights can be cold, especially in July and August. Summers are hot with temperatures ranging from 20-32 degrees Celsius. The rainy season is from October to April with heavy thunderstorms often occurring in the afternoon. Skukuza receives 553 mm of rain per year on average.

History:

Originally named Sabie Bridge, Skukuza was established in 1898 as the ranger camp for the then Sabie Game Reserve, which was later joined up with the Shingwedzi Game Reserve in the north. The land in between was then amalgamated with the two to form one reserve.

The Sabie Bridge was built so that the Selati railway line linking Komatipoort with the gold fields at Tzaneen in the north-western lowveld could cross the mighty Sabie River.

Renamed in 1936, Skukuza is a shortened version of the original name which was Sikhukhuza, a name given to the famous first warden of the park — Major James Stevenson-Hamilton — by the local indigenous people. It means "he who sweeps clean" in reference to him successfully removing the locals and anyone else necessary to establish the reserve. The library in the camp is named Stevenson-Hamilton as a tribute to his 40 years of service to the park.

The camp served as a stopover for the railway, and it was the Major who first experimented with the concept of tourism by providing an evening bushveld experience to train passengers passing through. It proved to be a huge success helping to make Skukuza an international destination for tourists.

Eventually, the inevitable frequency of the hundreds of trains per week resulted in too many animal fatalities. As a result, it was decided to route all trains around the park, and so the last train, called the Selati 3638, passed through Skukuza in 1972.

The two train bridges stand in memory of this part of the park's rich history, as do coaches from the Selati 3638 that have been retired to the camp station and converted into a restaurant. Unfortunately, the restaurant is currently not operational.

Skukuza

The first tourist huts were built at Skukuza in 1928, the year after the park was opened to tourists. One of the huts is preserved in memory of the camp's history and is now a popular visitor attraction.

During the following years the camp grew rapidly, adding hundreds of accommodation units, ablution and laundry buildings, restaurants, an auditorium, a shop, banks, car rental offices, swimming pools, a petrol station, conference centres, a museum and library and other infrastructure required to maintain its function as administrative headquarters for the entire park.

Amenities and services overview:

Reception and information centre: This is where you will check in on arrival, make reservation changes, book game drives and walks, report potential problems, as well as obtain travel and recent information on animal sightings. &

- Shaded game viewing deck overlooking the Sabie River &
- Field Guide-accompanied walks
- Open-vehicle, Field Guide-accompanied game drives &
- A la carte restaurant &
- Coffee shop for light snacks and drinks &
- Field Guide-accompanied, restaurant-catered bush braais &
- A large grocery, curio, refreshment, and general provision convenience shop &
- Coin-operated laundromats
- Petrol station &
- Communal kitchens with urns of boiling water, cook tops, wash basins with hot and cold running water, and electrical plugs are included &
- Accommodation servicing (bedding, cleaning, towels, soap, sweeping)
- Communal ablution facilities for campers, with baths, showers, and toilets &
- Two swimming pools with a separate paddling pool for toddlers &
- A small children's play area next to the restaurant &
- Riverside walkway with benches under shade trees &
- Crockery and cutlery hampers for hire
- Basic first-aid assistance for minor scrapes and accidents
- A doctor's office located behind the west swimming pool &
- Separate picnic area with swimming pool for day visitors, 4 KM outside the camp &
- Limited cable television in the guest houses and family bungalows only
- Free Wi-Fi access at the restaurant and in front of the coffee shop &
- Cell phone reception
- Limited emergency road service
- Motor garage with workshop &
- A beautiful church located in the staff village &
- Post office for mailing wildlife postcards to friends back home &
- A bank &
- Car rental desk &
- Educational wildlife movies shown in the auditorium during the evenings &
- Auditorium and conference facilities &
- Children's educational programmes &
- Educational centre/museum and library &
- A spectacular, par 72, 9-hole golf course, 3 KM from the camp &
- TV in the golf course bar &
- Car wash &
- ATM &
- Power points for campers
- Indigenous plant nursery, 5 KM outside the camp &
- One of the best bird hides in the park, 4 KM from the camp &

Church

Shady walkways overlooking the river

Viewing deck

Post office, bank and ATM

Restaurant: ♿

Skukuza currently has one large a la carte restaurant — the *Cattle Baron* — which overlooks the Sabie River. Large windows allow guests to enjoy the view in an air-conditioned environment, or they can dine on the open-air patio deck. The buffet-style breakfast is not to be missed, nor should their famous steaks and venison dishes which are served until 9.00 pm daily. There is also an adjoining coffee/take away shop that offers cakes, light meals and drinks.

For extreme African-atmosphere dining seekers, there is also the opportunity to experience a restaurant-catered bush braai outside the camp, in the wild.

TIP: This restaurant holds a unique opportunity for parents to enjoy a meal on the deck, overlooking the Sabie River, while keeping an eye on their kids playing safely on the playing equipment, only metres away.

The Cattle Baron restaurant deck overlooking the Sabie River

Cattle Baron restaurant interior

Outdoor dining on the deck overlooking the river

Children's play area

Breakfast buffet

TIP: Only 3 KM from the camp, the golf course restaurant offers lunches and a legendary breakfast.

Shop: ♿

The Skukuza shop is the largest in the park and is well stocked with everything that will make a visitor's stay comfortable and enjoyable. Included are souvenirs, books, camping and cooking accessories, firewood, food and drinks, snacks and ice cream, clothing, safari and camera accessories.

Skukuza shop

Day visitors' picnic site: &

Skukuza has a popular separate picnic and recreation area for day visitors 4 KM from the main camp. Designed to enhance the bush atmosphere, this picnic site is the largest in the park. It offers a large swimming pool with plenty of picnic tables, shady braai sites, and views of the Sabie River. A take away shop provides refreshments and picnic essentials, including skottel rentals.

Braai at Skukuza day visitors' site

Swimming pool area Skukuza day visitors' site

Things to do:

- Field Guide-accompanied bush walks
- Field Guide-accompanied open-vehicle game drives &
- The Metsi Metsi, Field Guide-accompanied overnight trail
- James Stevenson-Hamilton Library, museum and educational centre exhibition &
- Restaurant-catered evening bush braais &
- Educational programmes for children &
- View traditional dancing by special arrangement &
- Educational wildlife documentaries shown at night in the auditorium &
- Two swimming pools, surrounded by lawns and benches under shade trees &
- Play area with equipment for small children next to the restaurant &
- A round of golf or dine at the spectacular par 72, 9-hole golf course 3 KM outside the camp &
- Bird watching at the Lake Panic Bird Hide, 4 KM outside the camp &
- Visit the indigenous plant nursery, 5 KM outside the camp &
- Watch sport on the TV in the golf course bar &
- Visit the church in the Skukuza staff village

CAUTION: Only overnight visitors are allowed to access or walk around the accommodation areas.

21-seater game drive vehicle

Petrol station and car wash

Activity prices (Children half price)						
Activity	**Duration**	**Price**	**Min/max age**	**Departs**	**Includes**	**Min/max**
Sunrise drive	3 hours	R282	6/- years	4.00 am – 5.00 am	-	4/21 people
Morning walk and drive	4 hours	R535	12/65 years	4.00 am – 5.00 am	Snack, water	2/8 people
Afternoon walk	2.5 hours	R425	12/65 years	3.30 pm – 4.30 am	Snack, water	2/8 people
Sunset drive	3 hours	R300	6/- years	4.30 pm	-	4/21 people
Bush braai	3 hours	R767	6/- years	4.45 pm	Dinner	6/- people
Night drive	2 hours	R240	6/- years	8.00 pm	-	4/21 people

Visit www.SANParks.org or contact camp reception for exact times, prices, and details, or follow this web link directly to the Skukuza tariffs page: http://bit.ly/Skukuza-Camp

TIP: Skukuza accommodates many visitors. If you enjoy being first out of the camp in the morning, then you will want to be at the camp gate at least 45 minutes before opening time.

In-camp suggested walks: &

Unlike other camps, Skukuza has no perimeter walk. However, it does have a river walkway that leads from the restaurant past the riverfront bungalows. Also, the camp is large and has an extensive maze of roads which lead in and out of the various accommodation and communal areas as well as the campsite. However, please note that most of these areas can only be accessed by overnight visitors.

With an abundance of birdlife, beautiful landscaping and views of the Sabie River to admire, as well as interesting historical points of interest, a walk around Skukuza is well worth it. Follow the author-suggested route outlined in the *Accommodation Overview Map* and allow an hour or two to see everything.

Riverside walkway

Many meandering camp roads for walking

See the historical clock tower while walking

Museum: &

Standing in the centre of the camp is the famous Stevenson-Hamilton Memorial Centre, consisting of a reference library and an interesting museum. Here visitors can learn about the history of the indigenous people of the area as well as legendary African Rangers that helped to maintain, steward, and develop one of the world's greatest national parks. On display are also interesting exhibits of some of the park's diverse fauna and flora.

The skin of the lion which attacked Harry Wolhuter (one of the park's first rangers), who then single-handedly killed the animal with a knife, can also be seen here. The library contains a wide selection of Africana and books about the fauna, flora and history of the park.

Stevenson-Hamilton Memorial Centre

Interactive museum exhibits

Dog cemetery: &

Adjacent to the library, visitors can see Little Heroes' Acre, the final resting place for ranger dogs that died in the line of duty.

Each headstone tells a story of how a dog defended its owner to its death or provided warnings or diversions of danger from attack by wild animals.

Other dogs that died naturally after serving their masters throughout their lives are also buried in the cemetery.

Indigenous nursery: &

The very impressive Skukuza Indigenous Nursery is 5 KM outside the camp. Once the largest indigenous nursery in South Africa, it serves as a botanical research centre for the park and educational centre for visitors.

There are many tree species, shrubs, aloes and succulents on display, with signs that explain their typical habitats, growing characteristics and medicinal uses. The friendly staff are trained to answer questions.

Most of the plants have been grown from seed that were collected by rangers throughout the park. Of special interest is a boardwalk that meanders through a wetland, giving visitors a rare opportunity to view, on foot, the wildlife that lives in that environment.

Visitors who take the time to visit this unique nursery also have the opportunity to take a live piece of the Kruger park home to grow in their own backyard.

Nursery boardwalk

Indigenous plants for sale

The Oldest Hut: &

The first huts to accommodate tourists were built in 1929. The very first hut and toilet, named the "Campbell Hut" after W.A. Campbell, a founding member of the National Parks Board, still stands in Skukuza and has been restored to its original state.

Inside, visitors can see artifacts and original pieces of furniture that were provided for the comfort of guests.

Outside stands an old petrol hand pump that was used during those by-gone days.

Museum hut interior and furniture

The 1930s Campbell museum hut

Golf course: &

Only 3 KM from the camp, Skukuza offers one of the most unique golf courses in the world. Just imagine a 9-hole, almost 6,000 square metre course that can be enjoyed in and amongst the animals in one of the greatest wildlife sanctuaries.

There are no fences around the course. Players must sign an indemnity before tackling this par 72 challenge that is occasionally shared by baboons, warthogs, buck and more. While this might sound dangerous, no one has ever been reported to be hurt by an animal.

Established in 1972 for the park employees, and then made available to the public, the course is spectacular with an abundance of trees adding additional obstacles to the challenge.

Players can tee-off between 7.00 am and 11.00 am, and booking is essential. No caddies or golf carts are allowed, but trolleys are permissible. A bar that offers light refreshments is also provided on-site. Make sure to pack your golf clubs to take advantage of this close-to-nature golfing experience.

Camp trees: &

Skukuza camp has landscaped gardens with name tags on most of the larger trees. Some of the tree species that can be seen in this riverine camp are:

- Apple leaf
- Black-monkey thorn
- Buffalo thorn
- Cape ash
- Common cluster fig
- Common coral tree
- Eastern bushveld gardenia
- Fever tree
- Green thorn

- Jackalberry
- Jacket plum
- Knob thorn
- Knobby fig
- Leadwood
- Lowveld cluster-leaf
- Marula
- Natal mahogany
- Pod mahogany

- Red bushwillow
- Russet bushwillow
- Sandpaper bush
- Sjambok pod
- Tamboti
- Toad tree
- Tree wisteria
- Umbrella thorn
- Weeping Boer-bean

An ancient sycamore tree at Skukuza

Camp animals: &

Skukuza has its own resident population of tame warthogs. Some of the other species that you might encounter during the day in the camp are:

- Baboons
- Bushbuck
- Impalas
- Monitor lizards
- Snakes
- Squirrels
- Tortoises
- Tree agamas
- Vervet monkeys
- A wide variety of birds

Skukuza's resident warthogs

Some animal species that you might encounter in the camp during the night are the:

African barred owl

- Bats
- Cane rats
- Frogs
- Honey badgers
- Civets
- Genets
- Mongooses
- Nightjars
- Owls
- Scrub hares
- Snakes
- Spotted genets
- Bush babies

Camp resident vervet monkey relaxing and doing some human viewing

CAUTION: Take heed of the precautions about camp wildlife in the *General Rest Camp Information* chapter of this book.

Camp birds: ♿

Despite Skukuza being a busy camp, it supports an abundance of birdlife. A walk along the river from the restaurant terrace to the riverside bungalows is said to never disappoint bird watchers.

Depending on the time of the year and prevailing conditions, some of the species that might be spotted at Skukuza include:

- Ashy flycatchers
- Bat-hawks
- Black flycatchers
- Bronze manikins
- Collared sunbirds
- Dusky flycatchers
- Gorgeous bush shrikes
- Green pigeons
- Grey tit flycatchers
- Grey-headed bush shrikes
- Half-collared kingfishers
- Heuglin's robin-chats
- Lesser masked weavers

- Little sparrow hawks
- Mourning doves
- Orange-breasted bush shrikes
- Pallid flycatchers
- Paradise flycatchers
- Purple-crested louries
- Red-backed manikins
- Red-faced cisticolas
- Spectacled weavers
- Spotted flycatchers
- Spotted-backed weavers
- Woodland kingfishers

Woodland kingfisher

Game viewing from the camp: ♿

The Sabie River attracts many animals that can be viewed from the restaurant and river walkway. Depending on the time of the year and prevailing conditions, some of the species that might be seen are:

- Baboons
- Banded mongooses
- Buffalos
- Bushbuck
- Crocodiles
- Elephants

- Giraffes
- Hippos
- Impalas
- Kudus
- Leopards
- Lions

- Nyalas
- Warthogs
- Waterbuck
- White rhinos
- Wildebeests
- Zebras

Sabie River hippos

Conference facilities:&

Skukuza is a popular venue for conferences offering two centres to choose from — the Goldfields Auditorium and the Nombolo Mdhluli Centre that also includes five breakaway rooms.

Below are the services and equipment provided:

- Seating for 900 attendees
- Overhead projectors
- Rear projection facilities
- Laser pointers
- Microphones
- Screens
- Data projectors
- DSTV, computers and VCR
- Flower services

- DVD connectivity
- Slide projectors
- Roving and lapel microphones
- Wall-mounted speakers
- Poster boards
- Lockable safes
- Flip charts and stands
- Video projectors

- Photocopy services
- Fax services
- Translation booths
- Photography services
- Restaurant catering
- Self-catering allowed
- Sound equipment
- Electronic screens

Skukuza conference centre

Accommodation overview:

Skukuza offers 236 accommodation units consisting of 21 safari tents, 171 bungalows, 25 luxury bungalows, 1 family cottage, 14 guest cottages and 4 guest houses, plus campsites for tents and caravans.

In addition to a dormitory that can house dozens of learners and their teachers on educational visits to the Kruger Park, Skukuza can accommodate 745 guests in 240 accommodation units, as well as over 500 campers making use of their own tents or caravans. The camp has most of the facilities that you would expect to find in a small-sized town.

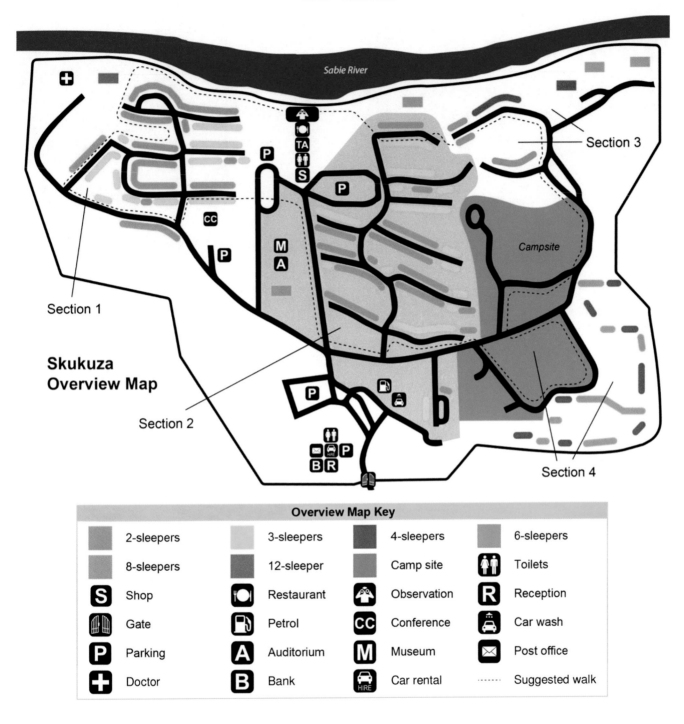

Skukuza
Overview Map

Section 1

Section 2

Section 3

Section 4

Sabie River

Campsite

Overview Map Key							
	2-sleepers		3-sleepers		4-sleepers		6-sleepers
	8-sleepers		12-sleeper		Camp site		Toilets
S	Shop		Restaurant		Observation	R	Reception
	Gate		Petrol	CC	Conference		Car wash
P	Parking	A	Auditorium	M	Museum		Post office
+	Doctor	B	Bank		Car rental	......	Suggested walk

Bungalows: (See Map Section 1 and 2)

Unlike most other camps, Skukuza offers a wide range of thatched-roof bungalows. Some are basic with limited self-catering facilities and no views, while others offer modern luxuries, well-equipped kitchenettes and en-suite bathrooms with river views. Kitchenettes include cooking pots, a frying pan, crockery and cutlery for four people, a bread knife, egg lifter, tin and bottle openers, and a water jug.

2-sleeper bungalow – Code LR2E

3-sleeper bungalow – Code BD3

3-sleeper bungalow – Code BE3

2-sleeper bungalow – Code LB2D

2-sleeper bungalow – Code BD2E

2-sleeper bungalow – Code BD2Z

2-sleeper bungalow – Code LR2E

2-sleeper bungalow – Code LR2E

2-sleeper bungalow - Code LB2

3-sleeper bungalow - Code BG3E

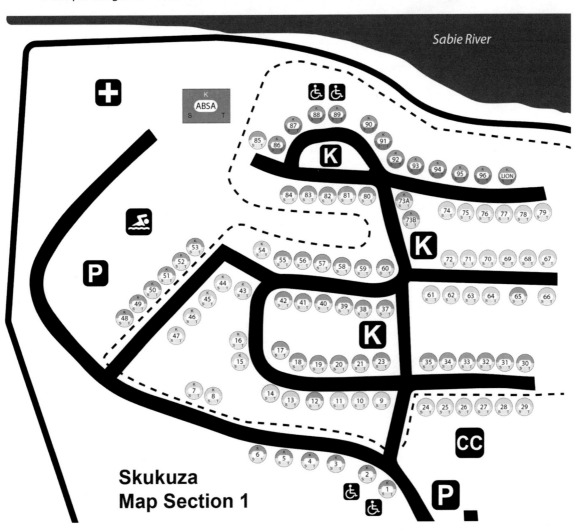

Sabie River

**Skukuza
Map Section 1**

Detail Map Key (Overnight-guest amenities)				
✚ Doctor	🅿 Parking	🏊 Pool	🅚 Kitchen	CC Conference

Skukuza

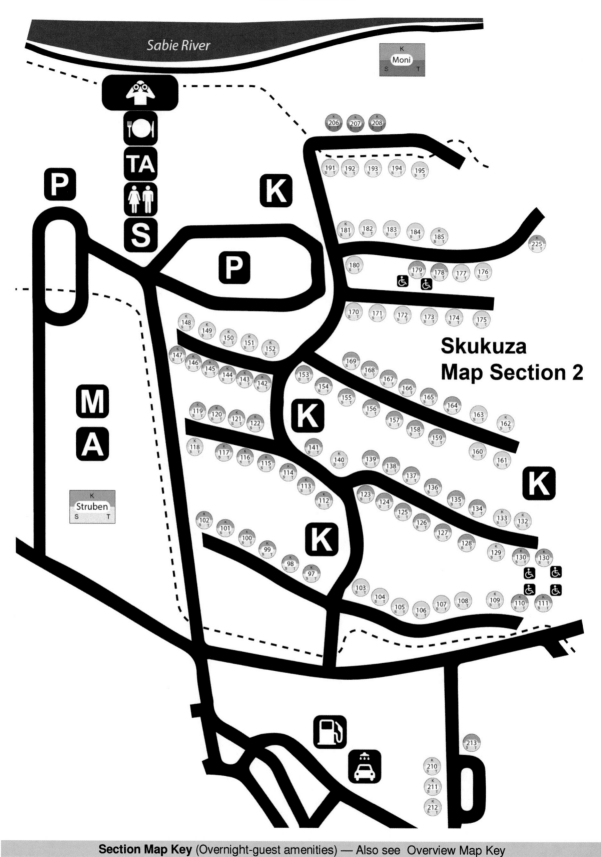

Sabie River

Moni

206 207 208

191 192 193 194 195

181 182 183 184 185

225

180 179 178 177 176

170 171 172 173 174 175

Skukuza
Map Section 2

148
149
150
151 152

147
146 145 144 143 142

153
154
169 168 167 166 165 164 163 162

155 156 157 158 159 160 161

119 120 121 122

118 117 116 115 114 113 112

141 140 139 138 137 136 135 134 133 132

123 124 125 126 127 128 129 130 130

Struben

102 101 100 99

103 104 105 106 107 108 109 110 111

98 97

213

210

211

212

	Section Map Key (Overnight-guest amenities) — Also see Overview Map Key			
K Kitchen	Ablutions	**L** Laundry	Pool

Luxury bungalow details (Map Sections 1 and 2)

Luxury bungalow icons	Unit (S T)	Unit (K, S T)	Unit (K, S T)	Unit (K, G)
Accommodation code	LB2D	LB2	LR2E	LR2W
Number of units	5	5	3	12 + 2
Wheelchair accessible code				LR2ZW
Riverview		-	•	•
Base guests allowance	2	2	2	2
Minimum base rate	R1,365	R1,365	R1,815	R1,815
Maximum base rate	R1,555	R1,555	R1,945	R1,945
Minimum additional adult rate	R410	R410	R410	R410
Maximum additional adult rate	R430	R430	R430	R430
Additional child discount	50%	50%	50%	50%
Maximum beds/people	2	3	2	2
Bathroom with shower and toilet	1	1	1	1
Closed veranda		1		
Bedroom with 2 single beds	1	1	1	1
Kitchenette		•	•	•
Communal kitchen	•			
DSTV – limited channels	•			•
Utensils	•	•	•	•
Fridge	•	•	•	•
Hot plate		•	•	•
Microwave		•	•	•
Sink/Basin	•	•	•	•
Air-conditioned	•	•	•	•
Electric points	•	•	•	•
Non-smoking	•	•	•	•
Wheelchair accessible				2

Visit http://www.SANParks.org to see detailed date-dependent tariffs and interior pictures of all units, or follow the below web link directly to the Skukuza tariffs page: http://bit.ly/Skukuza-Camp

Luxury bungalow numbers

LB2	48–51,53
LB2D	80–85
LB2K	52
LR2E	206–208
LR2ZW	88,89
LR2W	86,87, 90–96

Luxury bungalow location tips

Closest to the fence	85–96,206–208
Quietest	185,175–176,86-96
Best river views	86-96,206–208
Most private	85,53
Closest to pool	48–53
Closest to restaurant	148–152,170,180,181,191,205
Closest to shop	148–152,170,180,181,191,205
Closest to auditorium	29,30,147,148,118,119,66
Closest to the library	29,30,147,148,118,119,66

Standard bungalow details (See Map Sections 1 and 2)								
Standard bungalow icons	Unit	Unit	Unit	Unit	Unit	Unit	Unit	Unit
Code	BD3	BD2	BD2E	BE2	BE3	BG2	BG2E	BG3E
Wheelchair-accessible code			BD2Z				BG2Z	
Number of units	27	24	9	25	39	12+2*	20	15
No. wheelchair-accessible units			5				2	
Base guests allowance	2	2	2	2	2	2	2	2
Minimum base rate	R1,310	R1,400	R1,400	R1,065	R1,065	R1,135	R1,135	R1,060
Maximum base rate	R1,400	R1,400	R1,400	R1,290	R1,290	R1,290	R1,290	R1,205
Minimum additional adult rate	R240	R240	R240	R240	R240	R240	R240	R240
Maximum additional adult rate	R260	R260	R260	R260	R260	R260	R260	R260
Additional child discount	50%	50%	50%	50%	50%	50%	50%	50%
Maximum beds/people)	3	2	2	2	3	2	2	3
Single beds	3	2	2	2	3	2	2	3
Grab rail in shower and toilet			5				2	
Closed veranda			•				•	•
Bedroom with 2 single beds		•	•	•		•	•	
Bedroom with 3 single beds	•				•			•
Toilet and shower	•	•	•	•	•	•	•	•
Communal kitchen				•	•	•	•	•
Utensils	•	•	•	•	•	•	•	•
Fridge	•	•	•	•	•	•	•	•
Hot plate	•	•	•					
Sink/Basin	•	•	•	•	•			
Air-conditioned	•	•	•	•	•	•	•	•
Fan								
Electric points	•	•	•	•	•	•	•	•
Non-smoking	•	•	•	•	•	•	•	•

* Code for additional 2 units is BG2UT.
Visit http://www.SANParks.org to see detailed date-dependent tariffs and interior pictures of all units, or follow this web link directly to the Skukuza tariffs page: http://bit.ly/Skukuza-Camp

Code	Standard bungalow numbers (See Map Sections 1 and 2)
BE2	12,17,22,30–35,37–42,55–60, 65
BE3	9-11,13–14,24–29,61–64,66,67–72,74–79
BG2	123–128,213
BG2E	136–139,141,153–159,164–169
BG2UT	134,135
BG2ZE	178,179
BG3E	160,161,163,170–177,191–195
BD2	73A,73B,97–102,112–117,119–122,142–147
BD2E	3–6
BD2Z	1, 2,110,111,130,131
BD3	7,8,15,16,43–47,54,210–212

TIP: Be careful of walking barefooted on the grass in front of the riverside bungalows. The grass has a lot of thorns.

Guest cottages: (See Map Section 3)

Skukuza offers 13 guest cottages that sleep 4-6 people. Each has a choice of bed sizes and bathroom configurations.

4-sleeper guest cottage — Code GC4V

6-sleeper guest cottage — Code GC6DZ

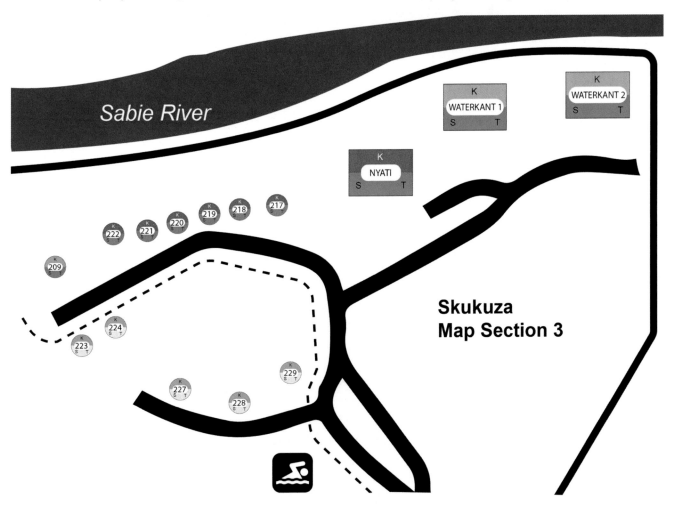

Guest cottage details (See Map Section 3)					
Guest Cottage icons	Unit	Unit	Unit	Unit	Unit
Accommodation code	GC4V	GC4VB	GC6	GC6D	GC6Z
Number of units	5	1	1	6	1
Riverview	•	•	•	•	•
Base guests allowance	4	4	4	4	4
Minimum base rate	R2,320	R2,320	R2,320	R2,32	R2,320
Maximum base rate	R2,420	R2,490	R2,490	R2,49	R2,490
Minimum additional adult rate	R410	R410	R410	R410	R410
Maximum additional adult rate	R430	R430	R430	R430	R430
Additional child discount	50%	50%	50%	50%	50%
Maximum beds/people	4	4	6	6	6
Single beds	4	4	6	6	6
Toilet with bath			1	1	1
Toilet and shower	2	2	1	1	1
Grab rail in shower and toilet					•
Bedroom with 2 single beds	2	2			
Bedroom with 3 single beds			2	2	2
Bathroom with toilet and shower	2	2	2	2	2
Bedroom with 2 single beds each	2	2			
Kitchen	•	•	•	•	•
Utensils	•	•	•	•	•
Fridge	•	•	•	•	•
Sink/Basin	•	•	•	•	•
Air-conditioned	•	•	•	•	•
Electric points	•	•	•	•	•
Non-smoking	•	•	•	•	•
Mobility challenged accessibility					•

Visit http://www.SANParks.org to see detailed date-dependent tariffs and interior pictures of all units, or follow the below web link directly to the Skukuza tariffs page: http://bit.ly/Skukuza-Camp

Code	Guest cottage numbers (See Map Section 3)
GC4VB	Elsie Clark 217
GC4V	218–222
GC6	209
GC6D	223– 225, 227– 229
GC6DZ	226

Guest cottage location tips (See Map Section 3)	
Closest to the fence	209 – 217, all guest cottages
Quietest	209 – 217, all guest cottages
Closest to pool	227 – 229
Closest to restaurant	209,223
Closest to shop	209,223
Closest to auditorium	209,223
Closest to the library	209,223

Guest houses: (See Map Section 3)

Skukuza has more guest houses than any of the other camps. All five of them are fully equipped with modern kitchens and amenities.

Some have a central communal lounge, entertainment area and kitchen with multiple detached bedrooms. All have large braai areas and four have unobstructed river views. Also, if you don't want to miss your favourite TV channels, then these are the units to go for as they include satellite TV, although channels are limited.

The Moni, Nyathi and Waterkant Guest Houses each sleep eight people in four bedrooms. The Wild Fig Guest House sleeps twelve people in six rooms, and the Struben Guest House sleeps six people in two rooms.

8-sleeper Moni Guest House — Code GMS

River and perimeter view from Monis Guest House

12-sleeper Wild Fig Guest House — Code GAB

River and perimeter view from Wild Fig Guest House

Waterkant 2 Guest House — Code GW2

View from Waterkant 2 Guest House

6-sleeper Struben Guest House — Code GSG

Guest house details (See Map Section 3)						
Guest house and family cottage icons	MONI	NYATI	WATERKANT 1	ABSA	Struben	WATERKANT 2
Name	Moni	Nyathi	Waterkant1	Wild Fig	Struben	Waterkant2
Guest house / family cottage	Guest h.	Guest h.	Guest h.	Guest h.	Guest h.	Fam. Cot.
Accommodation code	GMS	GNY	GW1	GAB	GSG	GW2
Number of units	1	1	1	1	1	1
River view	•	•	•	•		•
Base guests allowance	4	4	4	4	4	4
Minimum base rate	R4,310	R4,310	R4,310	R4,310	R2,320	R2,320
Maximum base rate	R4,620	R4,620	R4,620	R4,620	R2,490	R2,490
Minimum additional adult rate	R690	R690	R690	R690	R410	R410
Maximum additional adult rate	R720	R720	R720	R720	R430	R430
Additional child discount	50%	50%	50%	50%	50%	50%
Maximum beds/people	8	8	8	12	6	4
Bathroom, bath & shower	1	4	4	4	4	1
Separate shower	1					
Bathroom, Toilet & bath	3					
Bedroom with 2 single beds	4	4	4	6		2
Bedroom with 3 single beds					2	
Kitchen	•	•	•	•	•	•
Utensils	•	•	•	•	•	•
Fridge	•	•	•	•	•	•
Stove	•	•	•	•	•	•
Sink/Basin	•	•	•	•	•	•
Air-conditioned	•	•	•	•	•	•
DSTV (Limited channels)	•	•	•	•	•	•
Fan	•	•	•	•	•	•
Electric points	•	•	•	•	•	•
Non-smoking	•	•	•	•	•	•
Wheelchair-accessibility		•	•			

Visit <u>http://www.SANParks.org</u> to see detailed date-dependent tariffs and interior pictures of all units, or follow this web link directly to the Skukuza tariffs page: <u>http://bit.ly/Skukuza-Camp</u>

Safari tents: (See Map Section 4)

Skukuza offers 21 furnished safari tents at the southeastern corner of the campsite. Guests can choose from 2- or 4-sleeper units, with 4 of each facing the perimeter fence.

All include electricity, a fan, beds with bedding, a fridge and a small cupboard.

Each is slightly elevated off the ground on stilts and includes a small veranda, a table with chairs and a braai grill.

All of the safari tents are close to a communal bathroom, coin-operated laundromat and kitchen.

CAUTION: Units 300 - 305 look onto a maintenance building and an employee service path which detracts from the bushveld atmosphere.

2-sleeper interior safari tent — Code CTT2

4-sleeper perimeter safari tent — Code CTT4

Safari tent details (See Map Section 4)		
Safari tent icons	Unit	Unit
Accommodation codes	CTT2	CTT4
Number of units	12	9
Perimeter	4	4
Base guests allowance	2	2
Minimum base rate	R595	R595
Maximum base rate	R640	R640
Minimum additional adult	R160	R160
Maximum additional adult	R170	R170
Additional child discount	50%	50%
Maximum beds/people	2	4
Single beds	2	4
Rooms with 2 single beds	1	
Rooms with 4 single beds		1
Communal ablutions	•	•
Communal kitchen	•	•
Fridge	•	•
Fan	•	•
Electric points	•	•
Non-smoking	•	•
Wheelchair accessible		1

Visit http://www.SANParks.org to see detailed date-dependent tariffs, or follow the below web link directly to the Skukuza tariffs page: http://bit.ly/Skukuza-Camp

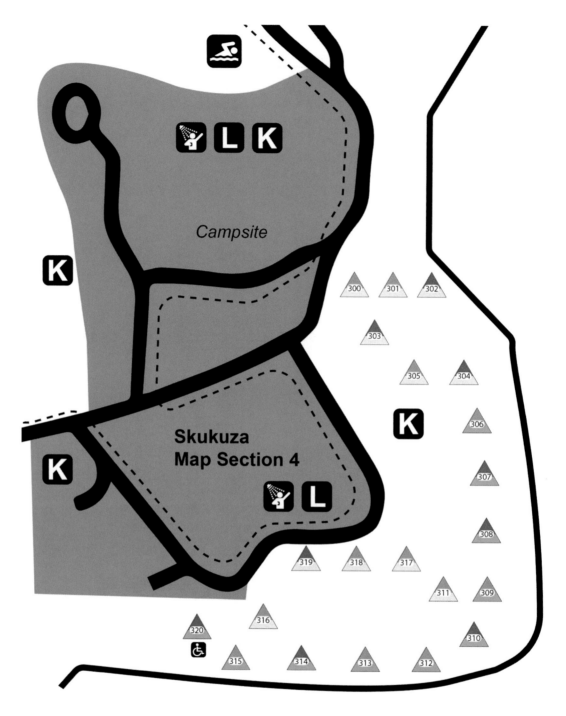

Campsite

Skukuza Map Section 4

Section Map Key (Overnight-guest amenities)			
K Kitchen	Ablutions	**L** Laundry	Pool

Code	View	Safari tent numbers (Map Section 4)
CTT2	Perimeter view	309,312,313,315
CTT2	Interior	300,301,305,306,311,316,317,318
CTT4	Perimeter view	307,308,310,314,320
CTT4	Interior	302,303,319,304

Safari tent location tips (See Map Section 4)	
Closest to the fence	306–315,320
Best perimeter view	310–315,320
Closest to bathrooms	316–319
Closest to kitchen	305–307
Closest to pool	300–303

Campsite: ♿ (See Map Section 4)

Skukuza has a medium-sized campsite located between the bungalows and the safari tent area. There are 85 partly demarcated and unallocated caravan and tent stands with power points.

When entering, campers have a choice of choosing stands in the interior section to the left, which is near to the swimming pool, or a limited number to the right, which are facing the perimeter fence. The interior stands are mostly on flat ground, while those at the fence are cramped and on sloping ground.

There are two communal ablutions, laundry and kitchen facilities with wheelchair access.

TIP: The ground does not drain well during the rainy season. If you are camping during the summer, choose a stand that is on higher ground.

CAUTION: Commercial safari outfits often accommodate their guests and run their operations from the circle in the dead end. Camping in that area can be noisy and busy.

TIP: There are not many shaded stands to choose from. Therefore, to find the right combination of shade and elevation, arrive early when campers are packing up and leaving.

Interior stands

Perimeter stands

Campsite communal kitchen

Communal ablutions

Campsite details (See Map Section 4)	
Campsite code	CK6P
Base guest allowance	2
Maximum people allowed	6
Minimum rate	R265
Maximum rate	R330
Min. additional adult rate	R82
Max. additional adult rate	R88
Additional child discount	50%
Visit http://www.SANParks.org to see detailed date-dependent tariffs, or follow the below web link directly to the Skukuza tariffs page: http://bit.ly/Skukuza-Camp	

More information and updates:

The author has been using and adding to his *Kruger Packing List* for more than 50 years. Now you can download your own complimentary copy of his all-in-one **Kruger Safari Packing List And Tips** by joining his mailing list (http://www.krugerkids.org/newsletter) to receive occasional newsletters featuring rest camp updates and news about the Kruger Kids project.

If you require more information about this camp, join his *Rest Camps of the Kruger Park Facebook Group* and post your questions or contact Skukuza Camp reception on 013 735 4196.

Additional information about the Kruger Park camps can be found on the popular SANParks Discussion Forum (http://bit.ly/KNPForum).

If you have comments or suggestions about this book, please contact the author at KrugerKidsSafaris@gmail.com or consider becoming a *"Meerkat" Book-Contributor* (http://www.krugerKids.org/contributors).

Pretoriuskop

Overview:

Pretoriuskop Rest Camp is situated in the southwest part of the park, only 9 KM from Numbi gate.

Known as Pretoriuskop Sourveld, the area consists of granite, an igneous rock soil, with a number of thickly vegetated valleys and beautiful low koppe/koppies (hilly outcrops). Close to the camp is an impressive granite dome called Shabeni Hill.

The vegetation surrounding Pretoriuskop consists of tall grass, known as sourveld, which is not palatable for grazers. However, browsers and their predators are plentiful and easy to spot on the roads that loop around the camp.

Dating back to the turn of the 20th century, Pretoriuskop is one of the oldest rest camps in the park. A repetitive best-run award winner, this medium-sized camp can accommodate more than 360 guests.

A variety of units, including basic huts to luxury guest houses and campsites, are offered. Facilities include bungalow and camping accommodation, a restaurant, cafeteria, shop and swimming pool.

Closest to Johannesburg, Pretoriuskop is also a convenient and popular destination for locals from the surrounding towns. Visitors enjoy this beautiful camp for its nostalgic historical atmosphere with its mix of large exotic and indigenous trees, as well as its popular part-granite rock swimming pool.

Pretoriuskop caters to the disabled and is also very suitable for families with children. Catering to such diverse visitor needs, budgets, and interests, it remains a firm favourite rest camp for Kruger Park visitors.

GPS co-ordinates:

S 25 10' 20"   E 31 16' 9"

Travel routes:

Route 1. From Johannesburg via White River: Take the N4 freeway to Mbombela/Nelspruit, then the R40 to White River, and the R538 to Numbi Gate and on to Pretoriuskop.

Route 2. From Maputo via Malelane: Take the EN4 to Komatipoort, then the N4 freeway to Malelane, to Malelane Gate and on to Pretoriuskop.

From	KM to gate gate	Drive time to gate	Park Gate	KM from gate	Drive time from gate	Route
Johannesburg via White River	391	4.25 hours	Numbi	8	0.25 hours	1
Maputo via Malelane	145	2 hours	Malelane	85	2.00 hours	2

Nearest airports:

Airport	KM	Drive time	Via gate
Oliver Tambo Int. Airport Johannesburg (JNB, FAJS)	376	4.75 hours	Numbi
Mpumalanga Int. Airport in White River (MQP, FAKN)	67	1 hour	Malelane
Mpumalanga Int. Airport in White River (MQP, FAKN)	42	0.75 hours	Numbi
Skukuza Airport in the Kruger Park (SZK, FASZ)	85	1.75 hours	NA
Maputo Int. Airport in Mozambique (MPM)	145	2 hours	Malelane

Please note that all travel times quoted are approximate and are dependent on weather, time of day, game-viewer cars blocking the road, and other unforeseen circumstances.

Check-in:

Overnight visitors must check in at reception which is immediately on the left when driving into the camp. The office phone number is 013 735 5128/32. The duty manager is Silindile Khoza who can also be reached by email at silindile.khoza@sanparks.org.

Climate:

Winters are sunny and warm to mild with temperatures ranging from 10-24 degrees Celsius. Nights can be cold, especially in July and August. Since the camp is located at a higher altitude than most others in the Kruger, it is also a few degrees cooler in the hot summer months with temperatures ranging from 18-30 degrees Celsius.

The rainy season is from October to April with heavy thunderstorms often occurring in the afternoon. Pretoriuskop experiences the highest annual rainfall compared to all of the other camps in the park, totaling 746 mm on average.

Amenities and services overview:

- Reception and information centre: This is where you will check in on arrival, make reservation changes, book game drives and walks, as well as obtain travel and recent information on animal sightings. &
- Field Guide-accompanied walks &
- Open vehicle Field Guide-accompanied game drives &
- A la carte restaurant &
- Field Guide-accompanied, restaurant-catered, bush braais &
- Grocery, curio, refreshment, and general provision convenience shop &
- Indigenous plants nursery &
- Coin-operated laundromats &
- Petrol station &
- Communal kitchens for campers and visitors staying in huts that have no cooking facilities
- Accommodation servicing (bedding, cleaning, towels, soap, sweeping)
- Communal ablution faciilities with baths, showers, and toilets &
- Swimming pool with a separate paddling pool for toddlers &
- Lawns with benches under shade, braai stands and picnic tables &
- Crockery and cutlery hampers for hire for camp cooking or picnics
- Basic first aid assistance for minor scrapes and accidents
- Separate picnic and braai area for day visitors &
- Limited cable television in the guest houses only
- Cell phone reception
- Limited emergency road service
- Post box for mailing animal postcards to friends and family back home

Restaurant: &

The *Wimpy* franchise restaurant is next to the shop. Offering light meals and a full a la carte menu, guests have the option of both air-conditioned indoor or outdoor seating. Take away meals are also available to visitors who prefer picnicking. For extreme African atmosphere-dining seekers, there is also the opportunity to experience fully catered bush braai dinners outside the camp.

Pretoriuskop Wimpy Restaurant

Inside the Wimpy Restaurant

Shop: ♿

Pretoriuskop shop is well stocked with everything to make a visitor's stay comfortable and enjoyable.
Included are souvenirs, books, camping and cooking accessories, firewood, ice cream, clothing, safari and camera accessories as well as snacks and packaged foods. Take away foods can be ordered from the restaurant.

Pretoriuskop shop

Pretoriuskop plant-nursery shop

Things to do:

- Field Guide-accompanied bush walks
- The Field Guide-accompanied Napi Wilderness Trail with overnight tenting - A four-day hike in the rocky landscape along the Mbyamithi and Napi Rivers
- Open-vehicle, Field Guide-accompanied game drives ♿
- The 42 KM Madlabantu (Man eater) 4x4 Adventure Trail ♿
- Restaurant-catered evening bush braais ♿
- Educational programmes for children ♿
- The Sable Trail in-camp walk
- Educational wildlife documentaries - Shown outdoors, six nights a week next to reception ♿
- Swimming pool adjoining lawns and benches under shade trees ♿
- Playground and paddling pool for small children ♿
- Many short game drives that loop around the camp, which are famous for rhino sightings
- Shopping for curios at the camp shop or for plants at the nursery ♿

Activity prices (Children 1/2 price)						
Activity	**Duration**	**Price**	**Min/max age**	**Departs**	**Includes**	**Min/max**
Early morning drive	3 hours	R282	6/- years	4.00 am – 5.30 am	-	4/21 people
Morning walk	4 hours	R535	12/65 years	4.00 am – 5.00 am	Snack, water	2/8 people
Bush braai	3 hours	R768	6/- years	5.30 pm	Dinner	6/- people
Sunset drive	3 hours	R300	6/- years	4.30 pm	-	4/21 people
Night drive	2 hours	R240	6/- years	8.00 pm	-	4/21 people
Napi Wilderness Trail Info: http://bit.ly/napi-trail	2 days 3 nights	R4800	12/65 years	3.30 pm	Meals	2/8 people
Visit http://www.SANParks.org or contact camp reception for month-dependent exact times, prices, and details, or follow this web link directly to the Pretoriuskop tariffs page: http://bit.ly/Pretoriuskop						

Expansive lawns and shady trees

In-camp walk: &

Marked by cemented sable and human spoor, the interesting Sable Trail winds its way through Pretoriuskop camp. However, please note that most of these areas can only be accessed by overnight visitors

Along the way one can stop and read about the trees, plants and points of historical interest, such as the royal huts that were built for the queen of England in 1947 which are still awaiting her arrival.

A brochure for the trail that gives more information about the stops as well as the wildlife that is often seen on the other side of the fence is available from the reception.

- Distance: 1.5 KM
- Climb: None
- Surface: Flat ground and lawn
- Shade: Partly
- Benches: Yes
- Toilets: Many communal ablutions
- Views: None out of the camp
- Opportunities to view game: Yes

This walk is an easy stroll over flat ground, with occasional benches to stop and rest. Allow an hour or two to take in all the information along the way.

TIP: Even if you are not a regular walker, bring your walking shoes. You will be glad that you experienced the Sable Trail.

CAUTION: Only overnight visitors are allowed to access or walk around the accommodation areas.

Museum: &

There is no museum at Pretoriuskop. However, being the oldest camp in the park, it is full of history, and in many ways is its own museum. To experience this aspect of the camp, one only has to take a stroll along the Sable Trail as previously mentioned. Along the way, there are many stops that include historical interest boards to read.

One of the stops on the Sable Trail

Camp trees:

Pretoriuskop has a magnificent collection of trees and plants. However, unlike all the other camps, many of the trees are exotic since the camp predates the decision to only allow indigenous varieties. Name tags on most of the larger trees and plants help visitors identify the different species.

Some of the indigenous trees that can be seen in the camp include:

- Black monkey orange
- Broom cluster fig
- Brown ivory
- Bushveld gardenia
- Cape ash
- Camel's foot
- Common cluster fig
- Common red milkwood
- Coral tree

- Forest fever tree
- Fever tree
- Green monkey orange
- Jackalberry
- Karee
- Kiaat bloodwood
- Lowveld chestnut
- Matumi
- Marula

- Natal mahogany
- Paperbark thorn
- Sausage tree
- Silver cluster leaf
- Umbrella thorn
- Weeping bushwillow
- Weeping Boer-bean
- White stinkwood
- White syringa

Black monkey orange tree

Camp animals:

Warthogs are often found feeding around the bungalows while the campsite is home to many guinea fowl. Some other animals that you might encounter during the day in the camp are:

- Banded mongooses
- Blue-headed tree agamas
- Chameleons
- Monitor lizards
- Elephant shrews

- Mongooses
- Honey badgers
- Snakes
- Squirrels
- Tortoises

- Monkeys
- Baboons
- Warthogs
- Impalas

Guinea fowl inside the camp

Wildlife that you might encounter in the camp at night are:

- Bats
- Bush babies
- Cane rats

- Civets
- Frogs
- Genets

- Mongooses
- Owls
- Snakes

Camp birds:

Pretoriuskop has plenty to offer birders. Depending on the time of the year, some of the species that one might see in and around the camp are the:

- African green pigeons
- Black cuckoos
- Black-bellied bustards
- Brown-headed parrots
- Gorgeous bush shrikes

- Green-capped eremomelas
- Mocking chats
- Owls
- Pennant-winged nightjars

- Purple-crested turacos
- Red-collared widows
- Redheaded weavers
- Retz's helmet-shrikes
- Scarlet-chested sunbirds

Game viewing from the camp:

Game viewing from Pretoriuskop is not an attraction since there is no river or dam view as there is in other camps. However, just like in any other camp, patrolling the boundary fence can often deliver unexpected surprises.

Impalas grazing next to the camp fence

Depending on the time of the year, some of the species that one can be lucky to view through and over the fence are:

- Baboons
- Duikers
- Elephants
- Giraffes
- Impala

- Kudus
- Lichtenstein's hartebeest
- Reedbucks
- Sable antelopes
- Spotted hyenas

- Tsessebes
- Vervet monkeys
- Waterbuck
- White rhinos
- Zebras

CAUTION: Use caution by not patrolling remote parts of the fence at night, such as the swimming pool area, and stay away from external trees that overhang the fence.

CAUTION: Remember to take heed of the precautions about camp wildlife in the *General Rest Camp Information* chapter of this book.

Accommodation overview:

Pretoriuskop offers 134 accommodation units consisting of 76 huts, 52 bungalows, 4 family cottages and 2 guest houses, plus campsite stands for tents and caravans.

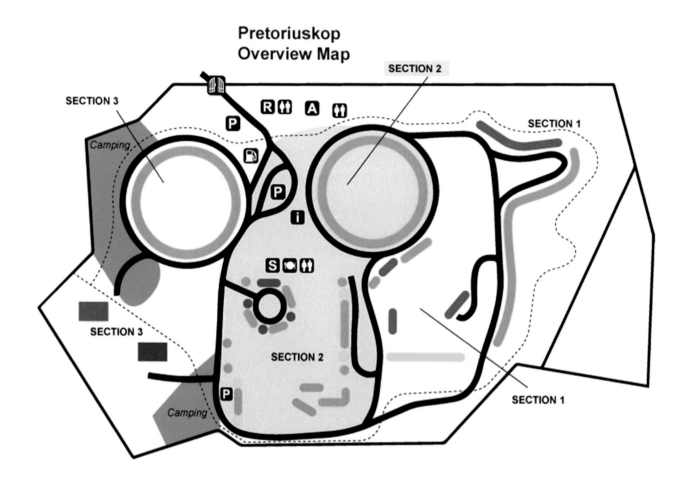

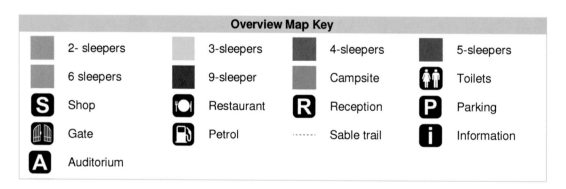

TIP: If you are going to stay in accommodation that relies on communal facilities, bring your own picnic hamper. It's much more convenient and you will have everything that you need in it.

2-sleeper bungalows overlooking lawn and the pool area - Code BD2V

Bungalows: (See Map Sections 1 & 3)

Pretoriuskop offers 52 fully serviced 2, 4 or 6-sleeper bungalows. Some face inside a circle of units, while others face expansive lawns and the perimeter fence. Most have self-catering kitchenettes while some offer communal kitchens. All consist of one room, a toilet and shower, plus a veranda where guests can eat or simply relax. Kitchenettes include cooking pots, a frying pan, crockery and cutlery for four people, a bread knife, egg lifter, tin and bottle openers, and a water jug.

6-sleeper bungalow - Code BG6

2-sleeper bungalow - Code BG2

2-sleeper bungalow with wheelchair access - Code BD2Z

2-sleeper bungalow perimeter view - Code BD2Z

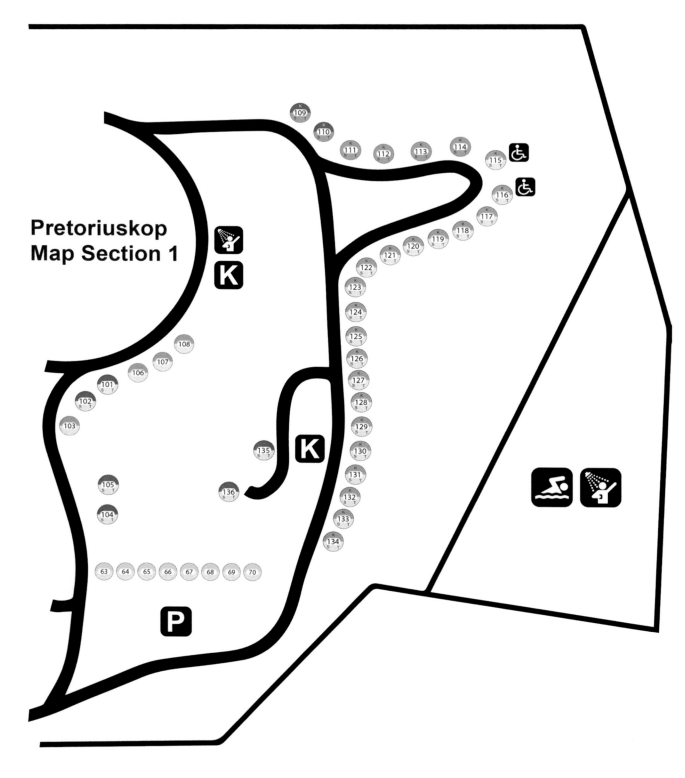

**Pretoriuskop
Map Section 1**

Section Map Key (overnight-guest amenities)			
K Kitchen	Ablutions	**P** Parking	Pool

Bungalow details (See Map Sections 1 & 3)

Bungalow icons	Unit	Unit	Unit	Unit	Unit	Unit
Bungalow codes	BD2	BD2M	BG2	BG4	BG6	FU4D
Wheelchair accessible codes	BD2Z					
Number of units	28	14	13	4	2	2
No. of wheelchair accessible units	2					
Perimeter	2					2
Base rate number of people	2	2	2	2	2	4
Minimum base rate	R1,120	R1,165	R985	R985	R1,060	R2,320
Maximum base rate	R1,415	R1,415	R1,245	R1,245	R1,330	R2,490
Minimum additional adult rate	R240	R240	R240	R240	R240	R240
Maximum additional adult rate	R260	R260	R260	R260	R260	R260
Additional child discount	50%	50%	50%	50%	50%	50%
Maximum beds/people	2	2	2	4	6	4
Codes for bungalows with double beds	BD2D		BG2D			FU4D
Single beds	2	2	2	4	6	2
Toilet with shower or bath					1	
Toilet and bath						1
Toilet and shower	1	1	1	1		1
Bedroom with 2 single beds	•	•	•			1
Bedroom with 3 single beds					2	
Bedroom with 4 single beds				•		
Bedroom with 1 double bed						1
Toilet and shower	•	•	•	•	•	•
Kitchenette on veranda		•				
Kitchen		•				•
Communal kitchen			•	•	•	
Utensils	•	•				
Fridge	•	•	•	•	•	•
Hot plate	•					
Sink/Basin	•	•	•	•	•	•
Air-conditioned	•	•	•	•	•	•
Fan						
Electric points	•	•	•	•	•	•
Non Smoking	•	•	•	•	•	•

Visit http://www.SANParks.org to see detailed date-dependent tariffs and interior pictures of all units, or follow this web link directly to the Pretoriuskop tariffs page: http://bit.ly/Pretoriuskop

Code	Bungalow numbers (See Map Sections 1 & 3)
BD2	117–129
BD2M	4–15
BG2	2,16–26
BG4	104–105, 35,136
BG6	40,55
FU4D	109,110
BG2D	1
BD2D	130–134
BD2MZ	3
BD2Z	115,116

Bungalow location tips	
(See Map Sections 1 & 3)	
Closest to the fence	115,116
Quietest	115–120
Closest to pool	115–134
Closest to restaurant	101,102,22–26
Close to shop	1–3
Closest to auditorium	1–5

Huts: (See Map Section 1 & 2)

Pretoriuskop offers 76 fully serviced 2, 5 or 6-sleeper rustic huts. Most are detached and face inside a circle of huts, while others are attached in rows. All huts consist of one room, a basin, fridge, air-conditioner and the use of communal kitchens and bathrooms.

2-sleeper free-standing hut – Code EB2

3-sleeper attached huts – Code EB3

5-sleeper free-standing hut – Code EB5

2-sleeper attached huts – Code EB2

Communal ablution building

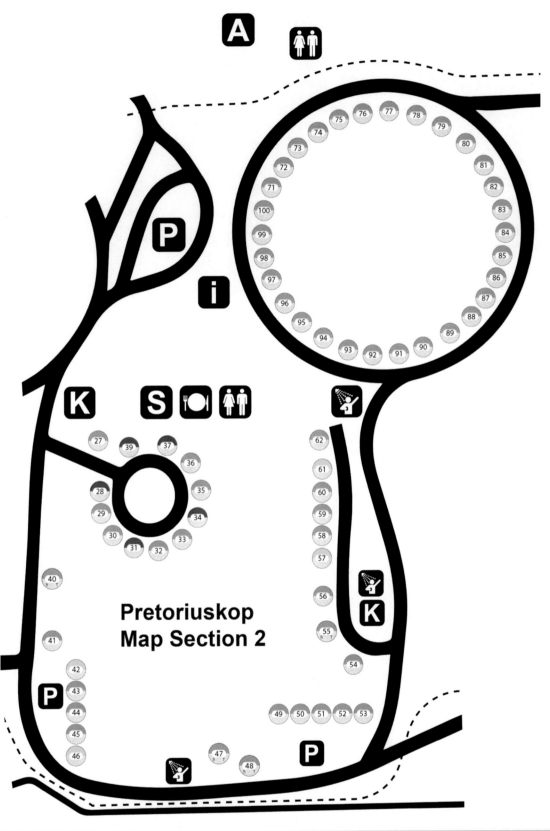

**Pretoriuskop
Map Section 2**

Section Map Key (Overnight-guest amenities) — Also see Overview Map Key

| **K** Kitchen | **Ablutions** | **S** Shop | **Restaurant** |

Pretoriuskop

Hut details (See Map Section 1 & 2)					
Hut codes	Unit	Unit	Unit	Unit	Unit
Hut code	ES2	EB2	EB3	EB5	EB6
Number of units	30	27	14	3	2
Base rate number of people	2	2	2	2	2
Minimum base rate	R350	R520	R520	R520	R520
Maximum base rate	R430	R640	R640	R640	R640
Minimum additional adult rate	R160	R160	R160	R160	R160
Maximum additional adult rate	R170	R170	R170	R170	R170
Additional child discount	50%	50%	50%	50%	50%
Maximum beds/people	2	2	3	5	6
Single beds	2	2	3	5	6
Bedroom with 2 single beds	1	1			
Bedroom with 3 single beds			1		
Bedroom with 5 single beds				1	
Bedroom with 6 single beds					1
Communal ablutions	•	•	•	•	•
Communal kitchen	•	•	•	•	•
Fridge		•	•	•	•
Sink/Basin					
Air-conditioned		•	•	•	•
Fan	•				
Electric points	•	•	•	•	•
Non-Smoking	•	•	•	•	•

Visit http://www.SANParks.org to see detailed date-dependent tariffs and interior pictures of all units, or follow this web link directly to the Pretoriuskop tariffs page: http://bit.ly/Pretoriuskop

Code	Hut numbers (See Map Section1 and 2)
ES2	71–100
EB2	27,29,30,32,33,35,36,39,41,43–45,50–52,54,56,58–60,62
	101-103,106–108
EB3	42,46,49,53,57,6,63–70
EB5	28,31,34
EB6	47–48

Hut location tips (See Map Section 1 & 2)	
Closest to the fence	44–53,75–79
Closest to the ablutions	91–95, 54–62,103
Closest to pool	67–70
Closest to restaurant	93–99,
Close to shop	93–99, 36–39,27,62
Closest to auditorium	71–76

Family cottages: (See Map Section 1)

Pretoriuskop offers four 3-bedroom family cottages with direct views of the perimeter fence. One bedroom has an en-suite bathroom, while there is a second bathroom for the other two bedrooms. Each kitchen is equipped with a gas stove and oven as well as a fridge and freezer with all the necessary crockery, cutlery and cooking utensils for enjoyable self-catering.

6-sleeper family cottage – Code FF6D

Perimeter view 6-sleeper family cottage – Code FF6DB

Family cottage details (See Map Section 1)		
Family cottage icons	Unit	Unit
Family cottage code	FF6D	FF6DB
Number of units	3	1
Perimeter	•	•
Base rate number of people	4	4
Minimum base rate	R2,320	R2,320
Maximum base rate	R2,490	R2,490
Minimum additional adult rate	R410	R410
Maximum additional adult rate	R430	R430
Additional child discount	50%	50%
Maximum beds/people	6	6
Double beds	1	1
Single beds	4	4
Toilet and bath	1	1
Toilet and shower	1	1
En-suite bedroom with double	1	1
Bedroom with 2 single beds	2	2
Bedroom with 1 double bed	1	1
Kitchen	•	•
Utensils	•	•
Fridge	•	•
Gas stove	•	•
Sink/Basin	•	•
Air-conditioned	•	•
Fan	•	•
Electric points	•	•
Non-smoking	•	•

Visit http://www.SANParks.org to see detailed date-dependent tariffs and interior pictures of all units, or follow the below web link directly to the Pretoriuskop tariffs page: http://bit.ly/Pretoriuskop

Family cottage codes and unit numbers (See Map Section 1)	
FF6D	111–113
FF6DB	114

Family cottage location tips (See Map Section 1)	
Closest to the fence	All 4 are
Closest to pool	114
Closest to restaurant and shop	111
Closest to auditorium	111

Guest houses: (See Section 3 Map)

Pretoriuskop offers 2 large 9- and 16-sleeper multi-roomed luxury guest houses with perimeter views. Thatch-roofed rooms are detached from the main houses, thereby offering a greater level of privacy to guests compared to some of the guest houses in other camps.

Each air-conditioned room is en-suite and one is wheelchair-accessible. Guests walk to and from the rooms and the main house on paved pathways and lawn and between braai areas. The main houses comprise of a kitchen, dining area and lounge with cable television.

Pierre Joubert Guest House – Code GC16

Pierre Joubert Guest House – Code GC16

Guest house free-standing bedroom

Guest houses view of perimeter fence

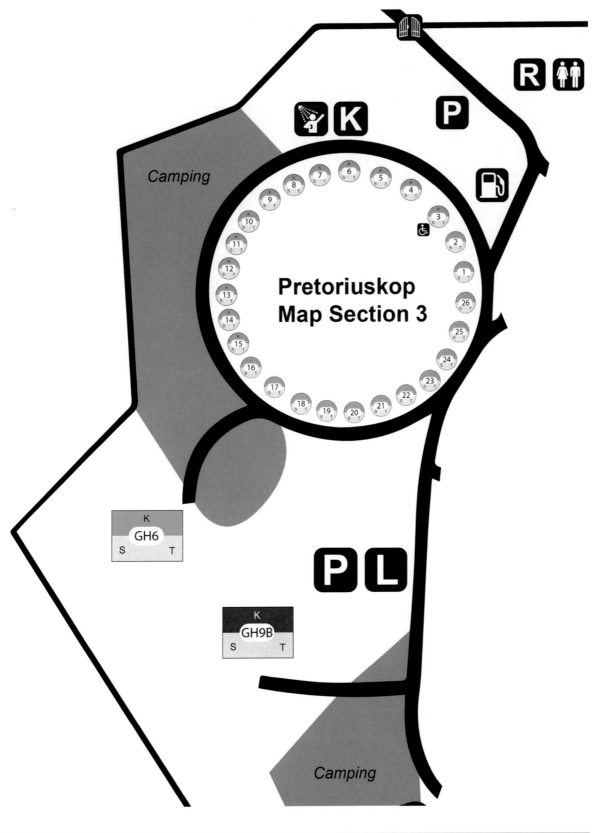

Camping

R P

**Pretoriuskop
Map Section 3**

| K |
| GH6 |
| S   T |

P L

| K |
| GH9B |
| S   T |

Camping

Guest house details (See Map Section 3)		
Guest house icons	K P. Joubert S T	K Doherty Bryant S T
Codes	GH16	GH9B
Names	Pierre Joubert	Doherty Bryant
Standalone units per group	4	3
Perimeter view	•	•
Base guests allowance	4	4
Minimum base rate	R3,775	R3,600
Maximum base rate	R4,620	R4,340
Minimum additional adult rate	R690	R690
Maximum additional adult rate	R720	R720
Additional child discount	50%	50%
Maximum beds/people	16	9
Single beds per unit	2	
Bench beds per unit	2	
Toilet and bath	1	1
Bathroom with toilet and bath		•
Bathroom with toilet, bath and shower per unit	•	
1 single bed		1
2 single beds	2	
1 double bed and 1 single bed per unit		•
Bench bed	2	
Kitchen	•	•
Utensils	•	
Fridge	•	
Stove and oven	•	
Sink/Basin	•	
Air-conditioned	•	•
Fan	•	
Electric points	•	
Non-smoking	•	•

Visit http://www.SANParks.org to see detailed date-dependent tariffs and interior pictures of all units, or follow the below web link directly to the Pretoriuskop tariffs page: http://bit.ly/Pretoriuskop

Campsite: (See Map Section 3)

Pretoriuskop campsite offers 45 demarcated stands in 2 areas, one on the north end, and the other on the west side of the camp. Map Section 3 shows the camp areas, marked "A" and "B", for the sake of discussion.

Each is serviced by a communal kitchen and bathroom. Some of the stands are not level, many are quite small and some are not shaded. However, if you get there early, you can secure an excellent perimeter stand.

Power points are provided, and there is a very nice coin-operated laundromat as well as washing lines between the two camping areas.

All of the stands are a short walk to the restaurant and shop, which are in the middle of the camp, but are far from the swimming pool, which is on the opposite side.

CAUTION: Baboons and monkeys are often active in Pretoriuskop. Follow the tips in the *General Information* chapter in the beginning of this book to make sure that these primates don't spoil your stay.

Area "A" 2-sided perimeter stand

Area "A" partly-shaded perimeter stands

Coin-operated laundry between the two areas

Area "B"

Campsite-stand location tips (See Map Section 3)	
Perimeter view stands	Areas "A" and "B" have good views of the perimeter fence.
Quietest stands	Area "B" sites experience the least activity.
Noisy stands	Area "A" is much busier than "B", and can be noisy.
Nearest to the ablutions	The stands closest to the gate in area "A". All are equally close in area "B".
Nearest the shop and restaurant	The stands in both areas are a short walk to the shop and restaurant.

Campsite details (See Map Section 3)	
Campsite code	CK6P
Base guest allowance	2
Maximum people allowed	6
Minimum rate	R265
Maximum rate	R330
Min. additional adult rate	R82
Max. additional adult rate	R88
Additional child discount	50%

Visit http://www.SANParks.org to see detailed date-dependent tariffs, or follow this web link directly to the Pretoriuskop tariffs page: http://bit.ly/Pretoriuskop

Nightfall at Pretoriuskop campsite

More information and updates:

The author has been using and adding to his *Kruger Packing List* for more than 50 years. Now you can download your own complimentary copy of his all-in-one **Kruger Safari Packing List And Tips** by joining his mailing list (http://www.krugerkids.org/newsletter) to receive occasional newsletters featuring rest camp updates and news about the Kruger Kids project.

If you require more information about this camp, join his *Rest Camps of the Kruger Park Facebook Group* and post your questions or contact Pretoriuskop Camp reception on 013 735 5128/32.

Additional information about the Kruger Park camps can be found on the popular SANParks Discussion Forum (http://bit.ly/KNPForum).

If you have comments or suggestions about this book, please contact the author at KrugerKidsSafaris@gmail.com or consider becoming a *"Meerkat" Book-Contributor* (http://www.krugerKids.org/contributors).

Lower Sabie

Overview:

Lower Sabie is a medium sized camp that lies west of the Lebombo mountains in the southeastern region of the park, close to the Mozambique border. Slightly elevated, Lower Sabie overlooks the perennial Sabie River. The surrounding area consists mostly of flat bushveld.

The most popular of all the camps, much of Lower Sabie's infrastructure is modern. A full range of accommodations are available, but only to visitors who remember to book well in advance.

To choose from in the main part of the camp are guest houses, family cottages, bungalows, huts and campsites with ablution and cooking facilities. Slightly upstream and apart, visitors can stay in fully-furnished and serviced luxury safari tents that are spread out and overlook the river.

Visitors love Lower Sabie because it is in the heart of one of the most game-saturated areas of the park. It is surrounded by good roads and well-frequented water holes which makes game viewing very rewarding.

A full range of family-friendly activities and amenities, such as a pool, the huge wooden viewing deck with a restaurant, and a shop also contribute to making this camp one of the park's top favourites.

With dramatic views of the river and expansive lawns shaded by majestic Sycamore Fig trees, Lower Sabie offers a relaxed, laid-back atmosphere to all who are privileged to visit.

The only downside to Lower Sabie is being able to reserve accommodation due to it being such a popular camp. However, even having the privilege of only being a day-visitor at this beautiful camp will be an unforgettable experience.

GPS co-ordinates:

S 25 7' 16"   E 31 55' 2"

Travel routes:

Route 1. From Johannesburg via Komatipoort: Take the N4 freeway to Nelspruit/Mbombela, to Komatipoort, to Crocodile Bridge Gate, and then on to Lower Sabie.

Route 2. From Johannesburg via Nelspruit/Mbombela: Take the N4 freeway to Nelspruit/Mbombela, to White River, to Numbi Gate, and then on to Lower Sabie.

From	KM to gate	Drive time to gate	Park Gate	KM from gate	Drive time from gate	Route
Johannesburg via Komatipoort	452	4.75 hours	Crocodile Bridge	36	1.00 hour	1
Johannesburg via Nelspruit/Mbombela	391	4.25 hours	Numbi	94	2.50 hours	2

Nearest airports:

Airport	KM	Drive time	Via gate
Oliver Tambo Int. Airport Johannesburg (JNB, FAJS)	473	5.50 hours	Crocodile Bridge
Mpumalanga Int. Airport in White River (MQP, FAKN)	118	1.75 hours	Crocodile Bridge
Maputo Int. Airport in Mozambique (MPM)	111	1.75 hours	Crocodile Bridge

Please note that all travel times quoted are approximate and are dependent on weather, time of day, game-viewer cars blocking the road, and other unforeseen circumstances.

TIP: Book early: Lower Sabie is one of the most popular rest camps in the park.

Check-in:

Overnight visitors must check in at reception and information desk in the main building behind the parking lot. The office phone number is 013 735 6056/7. The office manager is Bongile Louw, who can also be reached by email at Bongile.Louw@sanparks.org.

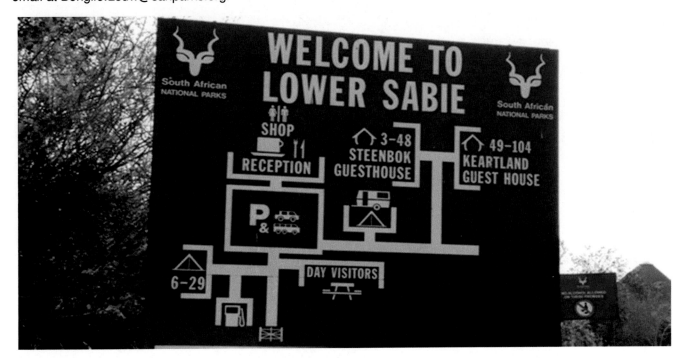

Climate:

Lower Sabie Camp enjoys pleasant weather all year round. Winters are sunny and warm to mild, with temperatures ranging from 7-26 degrees Celsius. Nights can be cold, especially in July and August. Summers are hot, with temperatures ranging from 20-32 degrees Celsius. The rainy season is from October to April, with heavy thunderstorms often occurring in the afternoons. Lower Sabie receives 625 mm of rain per year on average.

Amenities and services overview:

- Reception and information centre: This is where you will check in on arrival, make reservation changes, book game drives and walks, report potential problems, get travel information and recent information on animal sightings. ♿
- Wooden boardwalk/viewing deck with a restaurant and a shop overlooking the Sabie River ♿
- Field Guide-accompanied walks
- Open-vehicle Field Guide-driven game drives ♿
- A la carte restaurant ♿
- Cafeteria for light snacks and drinks ♿
- Field Guide-accompanied, restaurant-catered bush braais ♿
- Grocery, curio, refreshment, and general provision convenience shop ♿
- Coin-operated laundromats ♿
- Petrol filling station ♿
- Communal kitchens for campers, including urns of boiling water, cook tops, wash basins with hot and cold running water, and electrical plugs
- Accommodation servicing (bedding, cleaning, towels, soap, sweeping)
- Communal ablution facilities with baths, showers, and toilets ♿
- Swimming pool ♿
- Crockery and cutlery hampers for hire

- Basic first-aid assistance for minor scrapes and accidents
- Separate picnic and braai area with swimming pool for day visitors ♿
- Limited cable television in the guest houses only
- Internet Wi-Fi access for restaurant diners ♿
- Cell phone reception
- Limited emergency road service
- Post collection for mailing animal postcards to friends back home (hand-in at reception) ♿
- Wildlife documentary movies shown outdoors (depending on demand - check with reception) ♿
- Children's educational programmes ♿
- Power points for caravan campers
- ATM ♿

Outdoor auditorium

Shop, take away foods and restaurant area

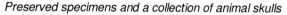
Preserved specimens and a collection of animal skulls

Shady lawns with views of the Sabie River

TIP: Don't forget your torches to enjoy walking in the camp at night. Lower Sabie is big, and there are many dark areas.

TIP: Lower Sabie accommodates many visitors. If, like the author, you enjoy being first out of the camp when the gate opens early in the morning, it is advised to be there at least 45 minutes before opening time. Rusks, and a flask of hot tea or coffee makes the wait more enjoyable.

TIP: Remember to fill up with petrol the night before an early morning game drive as the petrol station opens long after gate-opening time.

Lower Sabie swimming pool – right up against the fence, with lots of shade

Restaurant: &

The *Mugg & Bean* franchise restaurant is next to the shop and part of the large boardwalk/viewing deck that overlooks the Sabie River. Large windows allow guests to enjoy the view in an air-conditioned environment, or they can dine on the open-air deck, which is known to be one of the park's most spectacular dining experiences.

There is also an adjoining cafeteria/coffee shop that offers snacks, cakes, take aways and drinks.

For extreme African-atmosphere dining seekers, there is also the opportunity to experience a unique restaurant-catered and Field Guide-accompanied bush braai dinner outside the camp.

TIP: The restaurant's free Wi-Fi is accessible from the deck, but can be unreliable and slow during the day. However, it works perfectly after the restaurant closes at night. But remember to take a lamp, as the restaurant lights will be off.

Lower Sabie Mugg & Bean Restaurant

Restaurant deck overlooking the Sabie River

Lower Sabie Mugg & Bean restaurant deck leading down towards the safari tent area

Shop: &

The Lower Sabie grocery, curio, refreshment, and general provision convenience shop is well-stocked with everything to make a visitor's stay comfortable and enjoyable. Included are souvenirs, books, camping and cooking accessories, firewood, clothing, safari and camera accessories, ice cream, drinks, snacks and packaged foods. Take away foods can also be ordered from the snack bar right next to the shop.

Well-stocked Lower Sabie shop

Day visitors' picnic site: &

Lower Sabie has a popular separate picnic and braai area for day-visitors adjoining the main camp.

Designed to enhance the bush atmosphere, it offers plenty of picnic tables with shady and intimate braai sites.

The nearby cafeteria offers take away foods, and the shop offers packaged foodstuffs. Skottels can be rented at the picnic site, however visitors must pay a fee to make use of this picnic site.

Things to do:

- The main attraction is game viewing from the boardwalk overlooking the Sabie River &
- The Sunset Dam only 1 KM away is also very rewarding for game viewing
- Field Guide-accompanied bush walks
- Field Guide-accompanied game drives for visitors older than 6 years &
- Restaurant-catered bush braais &
- Educational programmes for children &
- Wildlife educational documentaries shown in the evenings at the outdoor auditorium
- Swimming pool surrounded by lawns and benches under shade trees
- Nearby attractions include Mlondolozi picnic site, Sunset Dam, Lower Sabie Bridge, and the Thananyathi bird hide

Activity Prices (Children 1/2 price)						
Activity	Duration	Price	Min/max age	Departs	Includes	Min/max
Sunrise drive	3 hours	R300	6/- years	4.00 am – 5.00 am	-	4/21 people
Morning walk	4 hours	R535	12/65 years	4.00 am – 5.00 am	Snack, water	2/8 people
Sunset drive	3 hours	R300	6/- years	4.30 pm	-	4/21 people
Bush braai	4 hours	R767	6/- years	5.30 pm	Dinner	6/21 people
Night drive	2 hours	R240	6/- years	8.00 pm	-	4/21 people

Visit http://www.SANParks.org or contact camp reception for month-dependent exact times, prices, and details, or follow this web link directly to the Lower Sabie tariffs page: http://bit.ly/Lower-Sabie

In-camp suggested walks: &

Lower Sabie has no full perimeter walk as some other camps do, but the camp is large and has an extensive maze of roads and open spaces which lead in and out of the various accommodation and communal areas, a campsite and a remote safari tent area. However, please note that most of these areas can only be accessed by overnight visitors.

With an abundance of birdlife, beautiful landscaping and views of the Sabie River to admire, a walk around Lower Sabie is well worth it. Except for the safari tented area, the entire walk is wheelchair-accessible. Allow 1-2 hours to see everything on the author's suggested walk as outlined on the Accommodation Overview Map.

- Distance: 1.5 KM. Refer to the overview map to see the author's preferred route
- Climb: Minimal. There is a slight rise in the road, approaching the safari tent area
- Surface: Lawn, decking or paved, except for the sandy safari tent area and especially along the perimeter fence
- Shade: Partly
- Benches: Yes, but not in the safari tent area
- Toilets: Yes
- Views: Great
- Opportunities to view game: Yes

Perimeter fence section of in-camp suggested walk in the safari tent area

CAUTION: Walkers should note that only overnight visitors are allowed to access the accommodation areas.

Wheelchair-accessible paved walkway

Museum:

Except for some interesting preserved specimens and a collection of impressive animal skulls in the reception area, there is no dedicated museum at Lower Sabie.

Camp trees:

Lower Sabie is a well-foliated riverine camp. It has beautiful gardens and lawns under huge trees. A number of impressive tagged feature trees are growing in front of the riverside bungalows.

Some of the trees that can be seen in the camp are:

- Brown ivory
- Common cluster fig
- Coral tree
- Fever
- Jackalberry
- Knob thorn
- Leadwood
- Wild mango
- Marula
- Mock marula
- Round-leafed teak
- Sausage
- Silver clusterleaf
- Snuff box
- Star chestnut
- Sycamore fig
- Tree wisteria
- Weeping
- Boer-bean
- White syringa

TIP: Bring comfortable shoes and explore this extensive camp on foot to see all the trees.

Giant sycamore fig tree

Feature trees that can be seen in front of the riverside bungalows include giant sycamores, marulas, as well as a young baobab.

Camp animals:

Some of the animals that you might encounter during the day in the camp are:

- Baboons
- Bushbuck
- Ground squirrels
- Monitor lizards
- Snakes
- Squirrels
- Tortoises
- Tree agama lizards
- Vervet monkeys
- A wide variety of birds

Chacma baboon

Some of the animals that you might encounter in the camp during the night are:

- Bats
- Bush babies
- Cane rats
- Civets
- Frogs
- Spotted genets
- Mongooses
- Nightjars
- Various owls

Lesser bush baby

Camp birds:

Depending on the time of the year and prevailing conditions, some species that might be seen in the camp are:

- Blue waxbills
- Burchell's coucals
- Burchell's starlings
- Crested barbets
- Eagle owls
- Egyptian gooses
- Fiery-necked and other nightjars
- Fork-tailed drongos
- Giant kingfishers
- Grey herons
- Goliath herons
- Grey go-away birds
- Helmeted guineafowls
- Natal spurfowls
- Sunbirds
- Weavers
- Woodpeckers
- Various hornbills
- Yellow-billed storks
- African fish-eagles
- A variety of river waders

Grey heron

Game viewing from the camp:

Depending on the time of the year and prevailing conditions, some of the species that might be seen from the camp are:

- Baboons
- Buffalos
- Bushbuck
- Crocodiles
- Elephants
- Giraffe
- Hippos
- Hyenas
- Impalas
- Jackals
- Kudus
- Leopards
- Lions
- Monitor lizards
- Snakes

- Warthogs
- Waterbuck
- White rhinos
- Wildebeest
- Zebras

The perennial Sabie River attracts a lot of wildlife that can be viewed from the camp, which is located on a slightly elevated bank.

Game viewing from the restaurant deck at Lower Sabie is spectacular as an endless procession of wildlife comes to drink and hunt.

Some visitors have been lucky enough to see lion kills from the restaurant or their riverside bungalows.

Accommodation overview:

Lower Sabie's 276 accommodation units offer something for everyone. Visitors have a choice of furnished 2-sleeper safari tents in a remote setting, 2-, 3- and 4-sleeper bungalows overlooking shaded lawns and the Sabie River, and 1-, 2-, 3- and 5-sleeper attached huts without a view in the centre of the camp. There is also a 7-sleeper guest house overlooking the river.

When choosing accommodation, one should make a choice between either being close to the shop, restaurant and viewing deck (huts and bungalows in the central part of the camp), close to the swimming pool (huts, bungalows and a guest house on the eastern side of the camp), or a remote area (safari tents in the western part).

If budget is to be the deciding factor, the huts in the centre of the camp offer some of the best value in the entire park.

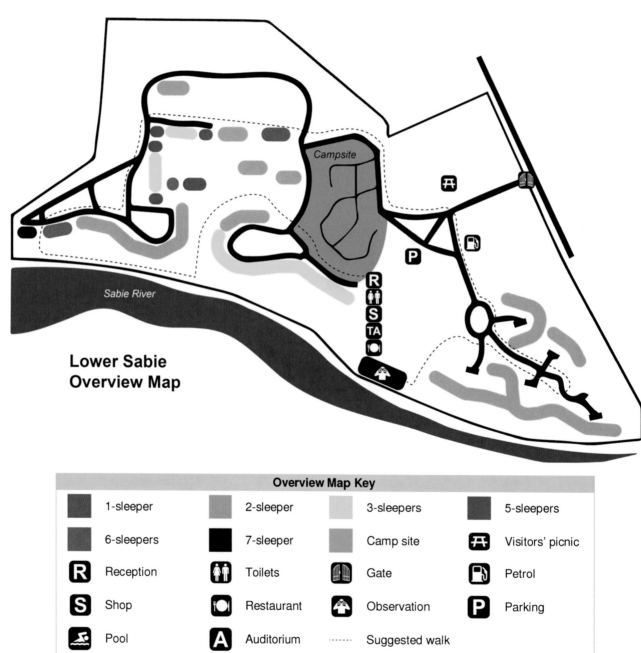

Lower Sabie
Overview Map

Overview Map Key			
1-sleeper	2-sleeper	3-sleepers	5-sleepers
6-sleepers	7-sleeper	Camp site	Visitors' picnic
R Reception	**ii** Toilets	Gate	Petrol
S Shop	Restaurant	Observation	**P** Parking
Pool	**A** Auditorium	······· Suggested walk	

Bungalows, cottages and guest house: (See Map Section 1 and 2)

The bungalows at Lower Sabie are arranged in such a way that some overlook the lawn and the river beyond, while others overlook each other and the lawn between them. The 2-person bungalows are located closer to the pool, but further away from the main building with its restaurant and shop. The 3-person units are an easy walk to the main building, while some of them are a trek to the pool.

Nearly all the bungalows offer kitchenettes, a toilet, and a shower. They should not be confused with the huts, all of which offer communal facilities. Most of the bungalows also all offer private verandas with outdoor furniture and braais. Outdoor kitchenettes include cooking pots, a frying pan, crockery and cutlery for four people, a bread knife, egg lifter, tin and bottle openers, and a water jug.

A few non-view bungalows only offer communal cooking facilities. While the table below shows the current situation, visitors should contact the camp reception to confirm configurations as the bungalows at Lower Sabie are in the process of being upgraded.

The bungalows are nice for families because the lawn in front of them allow space for kids to run around and play.

Two 5-sleeper Family Bungalows are also available. They offer two en-suite rooms, kitchenettes, and private braai areas. However, these units are close to the huts and therefore do not have any views.

There are also two 4-sleeper Family Cottages which offer two en-suite rooms, a kitchen, veranda, and great views of the river.

Finally, the Keartland Guest house offers secluded private accommodation for up to seven people in three en-suite rooms, a full kitchen, lounge, and a veranda with a spectacular view of the river.

The family cottages and guest house are close to the pool but far from the main building.

3-sleeper bungalow with river view – Code BD3U

View from 3-sleeper bungalow – Code BD3U

3-Sleeper bungalow – Code BD3

Bungalow with wheelchair access – Code BD3Z

Lower Sabie

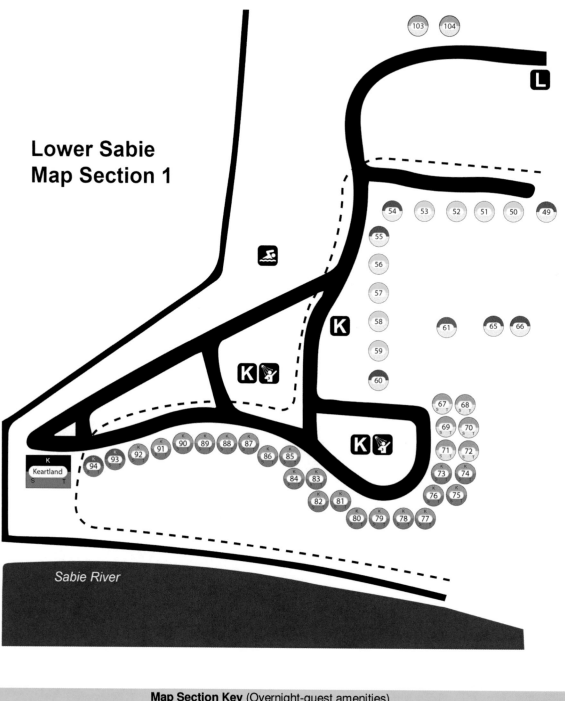

TIP: If you want a bungalow with a kitchenette, be careful when making your reservations. Older units offer communal kitchens which can be confusing as they are in the process of being updated. Check with reception before making your reservations.

Bungalows, cottages and guest house details (See Map Section 1 and 2)

Icons	Unit S T	K Unit S T	K Unit S T	K Unit S T	K Unit S T	K Keartland S T
Codes	BD2	BD2U	BD3	BD3U	FU4V	GKG
Wheelchair-accessible codes			BD3Z	BD3UZ		
Bungalow	•	•	•	•		
Family Bungalow						
Family cottage					•	
Guest house						•
Number of units	12	20	2	22	2	1
No. wheelchair-accessible units			1	2		
River view		•		•	•	•
Base guests allowance	2	2	2	2	4	4
Minimum base rate	R1,310	R1,395	R1,310	R1,395	R2,320	R4,310
Maximum base rate	R1,400	R1,650	R1,400	R1,650	R2,490	R4,620
Min. additional adult rate	NA	NA	R240	R240	NA	R690
Max. additional adult rate	NA	NA	R260	R260	NA	R720
Additional child discount	50%	50%	50%	50%	50%	50%
Maximum people allowed	2	2	3	3	4	7
Toilet and bath			•			
Toilet and shower	•	•	•	•	•	•
2 single beds	•	•				
3 single beds			•	•		
En-suite with 2 single beds					•	
1 bench bed					•	•
3 bedrooms with 2 single beds						•
Kitchenette		•	•	•	•	
Kitchen						•
Communal kitchen	•					
Utensils		•	•	•	•	•
Fridge		•	•	•	•	•
Hot plate		•	•	•	•	
Stove						•
Sink/Basin	•	•	•	•	•	•
Air-conditioned	•	•	•	•	•	•
Fan					•	•
Electric points	•	•	•	•	•	•
DSTV						•
Non-smoking	•	•	•	•	•	•
Wheelchair-accessibility			•	•		•

Visit http://www.SANParks.org to see detailed date-dependent tariffs and interior pictures of all units, or follow the below web link directly to the Lower Sabie tariffs page:
http://bit.ly/Lower-Sabie

Code	Bungalows, cottages, and guest house numbers (See Map Section 1 and 2)
BD2	25–30, 67–72
BD2U	73–92
BD3	32
BD3Z	31
BD3U	3–24
FU4V	93–94
GKG	Keartland
BD3UZ	15,16

Lower Sabie

Bungalows, cottages, and guest house location tips (See Map Section 1 and 2)	
Closest to the fence	77–80,18–20, 93,94
Quietest	93,94
Closest to pool	84-89
Closest to restaurant	1–4
Closest to shop	1–4
Closest to auditorium	67,68

Huts: (See Map Section 1 and 2)

Lower Sabie offers 1-, 2-, 3-, 4- and 5-sleeper accommodation units which they call huts. However, these older units are more like attached cluster rooms than traditional free-standing round huts.

All have single beds, a fridge, wash basin, air-conditioning, free-standing braai grills, communal bathrooms and communal kitchen facilities.

While the huts are very basic and offer no views, they are the most economical accommodation units in the park. The 3- and 5-sleeper huts are close to the pool while the 1- and 2-sleeper units are a short walk to the main building, restaurant, and shop.

1-sleeper hut – Code EH1

2-sleeper hut – Code EH2

Communal bathroom for bungalows and huts

Multi-sleeper hut – Code EH3, EH4 or EH5

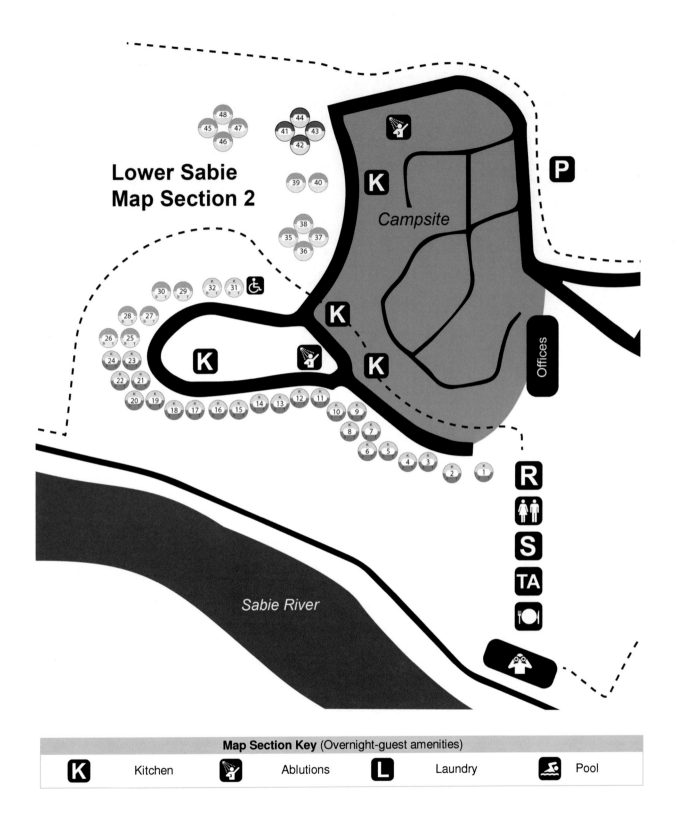

**Lower Sabie
Map Section 2**

Campsite

Offices

Sabie River

K P R S TA

Map Section Key (Overnight-guest amenities)							
K	Kitchen		Ablutions	**L**	Laundry		Pool

Hut details (See Map Section 1 and 2)					
Hut icons	Unit	Unit	Unit	Unit	Unit
Hut codes	EH1	EH2	EH3	EH4	EH5
Number of units	4	10	10	1	4
Base guests allowance	1	2	2	2	2
Minimum base rate	R360	R595	R595	R595	R595
Maximum base rate	R385	R640	R700	R700	R640
Minimum additional adult rate	R160	R160	R160	R160	R160
Maximum additional adult rate	R170	R170	R170	R170	R170
Additional child discount	50%	50%	50%	50%	50%
Maximum guest allowance	4	2	3	4	5
Single beds	1	2	3	4	5
Communal ablutions	•	•	•	•	•
Communal kitchen	•	•	•	•	•
Fridge	•	•	•	•	•
Sink/basin	•	•	•	•	•
Air-conditioned	•	•	•	•	•
Electric points	•	•	•	•	•
Non-smoking	•	•	•	•	•

Visit http://www.SANParks.org to see detailed date-dependent tariffs and interior pictures of all units, or follow the below web link directly to the Lower Sabie tariffs page: http://bit.ly/Lower-Sabie

Code	Hut unit numbers (See Map Section 1 and 2)
EH1	41–44
EH2	35–40,45–48
EH3	50–53,56-59,62–65
EH4	61
EH5	49,54,55,60

Hut location tips (See Map Section 1 and 2)	
Quietest	18–22
Closest to pool	54–60
Closest to restaurant	35–38
Closest to shop	35–38
Closest to auditorium	49,66
Closest to the bathroom	49,66,35–38
Closest to the kitchen	35–38,49,66

Safari tents: (See Map Section 3)

Unlike some of the other camps, the 24 stilted safari tents in Lower Sabie are positioned to maximise privacy. They are all located in a remote bushy part of the camp, mostly overlooking the Sabie River or western perimeter fence. The tents are furnished with two beds and fully fitted with kitchenettes, showers and toilets, a fan, fridge, veranda, and cooking utensils. The atmosphere is very different from the rest of the camp as there are no amenities and very little guest or staff activity. Two units are wheelchair-accessible.

CAUTION: Monkeys and baboons are a big problem for campers and bungalow guests in this camp. Make sure not to leave windows or doors open or food in their sight.

2-sleeper safari tent river view – Code LRVST2

2-sleeper safari tent – Code LRVST2

2-sleeper safari tent – Code LBVST2

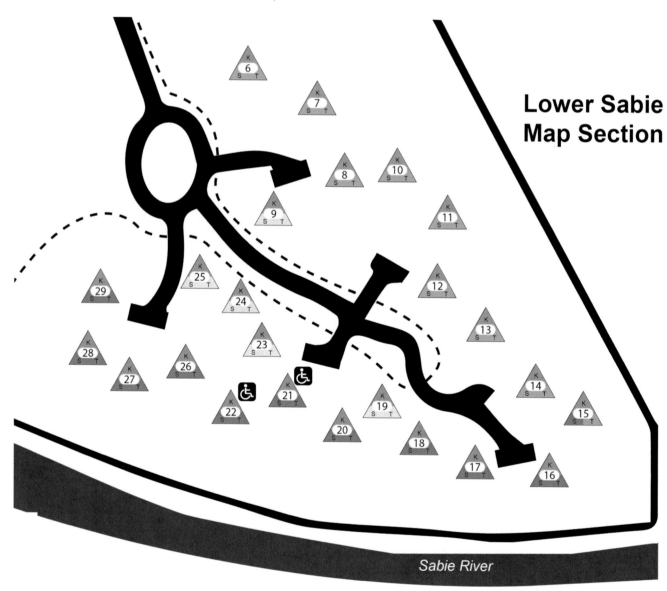

Lower Sabie Map Section

Sabie River

Safari tent details (See Map Section 3)					
Safari tent icons	△	△	△	△	△
Safari tent codes	LBVST2	LBVST2	LBVST2	LRVST2	
Wheelchair-accessible codes					LRVST2Z
Number of units	8	5	1	8	2
River view			•	•	•
Perimeter view	•		•		
Bush view	•	•			
Base guests allowance	2			2	
Minimum base rate	R1,250	R1,250	R1,250	R1,500	R1,500
Maximum base rate	R1,340	R1,340	R1,340	R1,600	R1,600
Maximum beds/people	2	2	2	2	2
Single beds	2	2	2	2	2
Toilet and shower	•	•	•	•	•
Kitchenette	•	•	•	•	•
Utensils	•	•	•	•	•
Fridge	•	•	•	•	•
Sink/Basin	•	•	•	•	•
Fan	•	•	•	•	•
Electric points	•	•	•	•	•
Non-smoking	•	•	•	•	•

Visit http://www.SANParks.org to see detailed date-dependent tariffs and interior pictures of all units, or follow the below web link directly to the Lower Sabie tariffs page: http://bit.ly/Lower-Sabie

Code	Safari tent unit numbers (See Map Section 3)
LRVST2 (river view)	16–18, 20,26–29
LBVST2 (bush view)	9,19,23–25
LBVST2 (river/perimeter view)	15
LRVST2Z (river view)	21,22
LBVST2 (river/perimeter	6-8,10-14 view)

Safari tent location tips (See Map Section 3)	
Closest to the fence	15,16–18,20,22,27
Best river views	15,16–18,20,22,27
Quietest	15,16
Closest to restaurant	28,29
Closest to shop	28,29

TIP: If spending time at the swimming pool is important to you, then the safari tents at Lower Sabie might not be your best choice, as the pool is at the opposite end of the camp. This means that you have to drive to get there.

TIP: Unlike nearly all huts and bungalows, safari tents are not air-conditioned. Staying in one is, therefore, most enjoyable during the cooler months and not very comfortable during the height of summer.

Campsite: (See Map Section 2)

Lower Sabie Camp Site is not very popular with campers. This is mainly because the 38 demarcated stands are small, and none of them have any views. However, unlike most of the other rest camps, the camping area is conveniently located right next to the main building which houses the reception, shop, restaurant, and the spectacular viewing deck.

The swimming pool, on the other hand, is on the east side of the camp and is quite a tiring walk when temperatures are in above 40 degrees Celcius.

The campsite is serviced by three communal kitchens and two ablution facilities. A coin-operated laundromat is also available.

All the stands have power, and half of them are shaded. Setting up is on ground that, although flat, is hard and stony.

CAUTION: Don't allow children to walk around with food in their hands, as baboons or monkeys could grab it from them, and bite them if they resist. Remember that both species are wild animals and can be very dangerous..

TIP: Bring steel pegs and a mallet.

CAUTION: This campsite does not drain very well and can, therefore, be quite muddy during the wet season.

Limited shaded camp stands

Communal bathroom

Communal kitchen

Level camp stands

Stand location tips (See Map Section 3)	
Closest to the fence	10
Closest to pool	3,7,9,19,20
Closest to restaurant	31,32
Closest to shop	31,32
Closest to auditorium	1,3,7,9

CAUTION: To deter thieving monkeys and baboons, lock all food away in the secure pantry cage that is provided with each tent. Alternatively, you can lock your food in your car boot.

Campsite details (See Map Section 3)	
Campsite code	CK6P
Base guest allowance	2
Power connection	•
Minimum base rate	R305
Maximum base rate	R330
Min. additional adult rate	R82
Max. additional adult rate	R88
Additional child discount	50%
Maximum people allowed	6

Visit http://www.SANParks.org to see detailed date-dependent tariffs or follow the below web link directly to the Lower Sabie tariffs page: http://bit.ly/Lower-Sabie

More information and updates:

The author has been using and adding to his *Kruger Packing List* for more than 50 years. Now you can download your own complimentary copy of his all-in-one **Kruger Safari Packing List And Tips** by joining his mailing list (http://www.krugerkids.org/newsletter) to receive occasional newsletters featuring rest camp updates and news about the Kruger Kids project.

If you require more information about this camp, join his *Rest Camps of the Kruger Park Facebook Group* and post your questions or contact Lower Sabie Camp reception on 013 735 6056/7.

Additional information about the Kruger Park camps can be found on the popular SANParks Discussion Forum (http://bit.ly/KNPForum).

If you have comments or suggestions about this book, please contact the author at KrugerKidsSafaris@gmail.com or consider becoming a *"Meerkat" Book-Contributor* (http://www.krugerKids.org/contributors).

Kruger Safari Packing List and Tips

The author has been using and adding to his *Kruger Safari Packing List* for more than 50 years. Now you can download your own copy of his all-in-one **Kruger Safari Packing List And Tips** for free by joining his mailing list.

Kruger Kids and *Rest Camps of the Kruger Park* is an evolving project. Join our mailing list to receive the following benefits:

- Receive our newsletter and watch us grow
- Get rest camp updates and news
- Be notified and receive a discount when our future book editions are published
- Download the author's *Kruger Safari Packing List And Tips*, so that you don't forget anything when you visit the Kruger National Park

Free Download at
www.KrugerKids.org/Newsletter

The author promises to never ever share your email address with anyone.

Bushveld Store

Here you will find everything that you need to make your visit to the Kruger National Park enjoyable. Included are cameras, binoculars, torches, guide books, maps, safari gear, and much more.

All prices are exactly the same as you will find when you go directly to buy online from Amazon.com. However, by purchasing via this store, our Kruger Kids project earns a small commission from every sale. If there is something which you need that you do not see here, please let us know so that we can add it to make this a great, one-stop for all of your Kruger safari needs.

Visit our store at
BushveldStore.com

South African customers please note that all goods are supplied from the United States or Europe and delivery is guaranteed by Amazon.com via private courier services. Aside from this benefit, and the advantage of a wide selection, comparing prices will more often than not reveal that they are most competitive.

In support of

Giving orphaned children the gift of a Kruger safari

About The Author

With wide eyes, excitement, and equipped with a Kodak Brownie black-and-white box camera, the author was first introduced to the Kruger National Park at the age of 12, when he joined a primary school excursion into the area.

Arriving at Skukuza for the first time, the rest camp atmosphere, sounds, sights and smells instantly captivated his soul. The idea of being in a fenced-in island surrounded by wild animals and the African bushveld was simply the most magical experience of his life.

As a young man, Marius Smook repeatedly returned to thoroughly explore the park and all of its camps with anyone who cared to accompany him to share the experience again and again.

As a father, there was no greater joy for him than to introduce the magic of the Kruger to his children. As soon as they could walk, he had them patrolling the camp perimeter fences at night in search of torchlight-reflecting eyes. He taught them to identify the cackling of hyenas, and the grunting of hippos as they sat around braai fires, and listened for the roar of lions late at night as they lay in their camp beds.

By establishing Kruger Kids, the author intends to extend the joy to children who do not have parents to take them to the Kruger. Safaris for small groups of accompanied orphans are intended to be financed by the sale of this and other volumes that he is publishing about the rest camps of the Kruger Park.

In conclusion, after spending his childhood in Pretoria, the author spent most of his adult life living and working in Durban and the United States. He now spends much of his time writing about and — now equipped with a digital camera — exploring the Kruger Park during the South African winter months.

Made in the USA
Las Vegas, NV
16 May 2023

72126346R00079